SEVEN STEPS TO
ELEVATING,
EFFECTIVE
LEADERSHIP

SEVEN STEPS TO ELEVATING EFFECTIVE
LEADERSHIP

REX TONKINS

credo
house publishers

Published in the United States by Credo House Publishers,
a division of Credo Communications LLC, Grand Rapids, Michigan
credohousepublishers.com

ISBN: 978-1-625860-91-0

Cover and interior design by Nick Mulder
Editing by Donna Huisjen

Printed in the United States of America
First edition

I am grateful to the Lord for inspiring me to write this book, as well as for the amazing support and encouragement of my wife, Vickie. My words have been influenced by decades of good, bad, and ugly experiences that have helped to mold me as the leader I am today. The fundamental biblical truths these experiences have revealed are applicable for every age group and every person who desires to elevate their leadership effectiveness.

CONTENTS

INTRODUCTION

The mantle of leadership fell on me early in my life, when I helped to organize a waterslide expedition for thirty-two peers, all under the age of twelve and all from the inner city. The miracle aspect of this unlikely expedition is that there were no adults to facilitate the journey across town. Learning of the opportunity through the local newspaper, I collected vouchers for all my peers, both boys and girls, and obtained permission slips signed by their parents for each child to participate in the great adventure. In addition, bus passes had to be collected for each participant to be able to ride the city bus.

Meeting in front of the home of my friend Anthony on Logan Street, we departed en masse, heading north to catch the city bus. We had to cross the four-lane Lee Street and navigate the hill to get to Gorrell Street. I remember looking back at the concerned and baffled faces of parents—mostly single parents wondering what I had just managed to accomplish. Just picture thirty-two inner-city youth around the age of twelve walking together without adult supervision. The sight was no doubt mind-boggling, particularly as the procession was orderly and respectful.

We arrived at the bus stop a few minutes before the bus, climbed aboard, taking up most of the seats, and stayed together. Our first stop was downtown to transfer to another bus to get to the circle mall on the northeast side of Greensboro. We then switched buses to head to our destination, the bus driver looking on with evident amazement. Thirty-two preteens on the bus, well behaved and following the direction of a young peer. Arriving at our destination, our group had to cross another, less busy four-lane to get to the waterslide.

Everyone was enthusiastic, this being the first waterslide experience for the majority of the group. On that day we established a happy memory of repeatedly running up and riding down the waterslide. Pausing to assess how my peers were doing, I felt the weight of responsibility to look after the well-being of each person.

In this moment of observation and introspection I realized that we were having the adventure of a lifetime. As I reflect back on that time as a young adolescent, my recollection of the laughter and joy on their faces remains priceless. The only sad thing about that day is that it had to come to end.

To eliminate the need to walk home I had to gather the group, make sure everyone was accounted for, and head back to the bus stop before the last bus run. Boarding the bus, we headed downtown to catch our transfer to Gorrell Street. Arriving there, we disembarked, our faces happy and our bodies still wet from the water slide. We walked down Logan Street and safely crossed Lee Street, a major thoroughfare, before arriving back to our Ray Warren neighborhood. Looking back, I recognize that this adventure was an incredible success, with no one lost or injured and no fights. I attribute our successful adventure to God's watching over and protecting us.

As my friend Butch Lee from Atlanta has stated, "No one can deny the mantle of leadership that is on one's life. A person may try to run from it, but it will always manifest in some fashion."

In this book, I am going to take you on a journey of discovery to help you identify qualities of true and real leadership. In addition, we will look into the lives of individuals who have demonstrated effective leadership attributes. Further, I'll reveal secrets that have profoundly influenced my own leadership journey. Before we dive into the seven elevating, effective principles of leadership, let's define the term. *Leadership* is the ability to influence and guide others to accomplish a desired mission by providing purpose, direction, vision, and motivation. The Greek *anax* refers to a tribal ruler, a king, or a military leader, while the Hebrew *nagid* points to a ruler, prince, chief, or commander. Leadership invariably entails change, which makes criticism inevitable for leaders because people generally prefer the status quo. According to Proverbs 25:12, however, criticism itself can be a value as good as gold: "Like an earring of gold and an ornament of fine gold is a wise rebuker to an obedient ear."

The greatest leader of all time is Jesus Christ, who has modeled for humankind the best way to lead people. Every leader should look to the Bible for guidance because it is the best model to follow for elevating, effective leadership. We all must face the reality that with leadership comes criticism and even persecution, especially if your leadership is in the area of pursuing godliness and righteousness. Effective leaders manifest a unique brand of thinking, look at criticism as an ally to help them see the bigger picture, and appreciate different perspectives. We must discern between the different types of criticism. Some well-intentioned people genuinely want their voices heard, while other criticism is deceitful, intended to destroy and tear down. Unfortunately, as a leader you will have to listen carefully to both types in order to understand where people stand with regard to your leadership. In the words of Rosalyn Carter, "Leaders take people where they want to go, but great leaders take people where they don't necessarily want to go, but where they ought to go." Dawson Troutman reflects, "Leaders must understand there is a kernel of truth in every criticism. Look for it and when you find it, rejoice in its value."

Jesus demonstrated effective leadership, and God Himself, in His own person, shows us the importance of working together as a team. The joint goal of the Father, Son, and Holy Spirit is to redeem humankind back to the Father. Since God is about redemption, our leadership should point in the direction of redemption with a holy God who desires relationship with us. Jesus poured His life into twelve leaders so that the message of salvation and hope could get out to humanity. The Holy Spirit helps bring the message with boldness and power, all the while offering comfort in difficult times. And our infinitely generous Father offered up His only begotten Son and continues to give gifts to the Church, His body, to help us be effective in advancing His agenda.

The Father is the author of life, Jesus is the redeemer of life, and the Holy Spirit empowers us with life. God clearly helps us see that leading is about assisting people, restoring people, and helping them find their purpose and destiny in Christ Jesus.

Now that we understand that God operates in our lives through a team approach, we must understand what is required of human leaders. As Micah 6:8 specifies, "He has shown you, O man, what is good; And what does the LORD require of you, But to do justly, To love mercy, And to walk humbly with your God?" These three foundational mandates are vital to God and therefore need to be important to us as well. In obedience, we need to endeavor to do what is right in God's sight, to deal with every situation in love and mercy, and to keep in the forefront of our minds that we are nothing without God and therefore need to walk in complete humility. No one likes pain, but, as Billy Graham points out, "leadership is forged in the furnace and leadership is a set of life experiences melded by intense heat." Every ounce of our character must go through this intense heating process to allow dross or impurities or selfishness or wrong motives to rise to the surface to be siphoned off, forming leaders with hearts of pure gold. Leadership is about learning from our mistakes and failures. Unfortunately, we learn more rapidly from painful experiences. "No Pain, No Gain," though clichéd, is so true! If we want to leave a lasting legacy, we must learn from the past to identify what has been effective so we can apply those timeless principles to today, allowing us to lead effectively in this millennium, which is in such dire need of leadership.

Jesus modeled leadership by ascending above all other powers and setting captives free. However, before our Lord ascended he first descended into the lower regions of the earth, to deal with hell, death, and the grave. Jesus also endured a brutal beating and was crucified so that all humankind would have the opportunity to experience liberation from the bondage of Satan, our adversary and accuser. As Paul reminds us in Ephesians 4:8, leadership involves action; it's all about going and being about the Father's business. Jesus, who endured pain and suffering on a rugged cross, (1) shows us that leaders will suffer, (2) descended into hell to set captives free, and (3) ascended with power and gave gifts to people so that the body of Christ might be equipped to serve effectively.

To be effective in our leadership we must follow Jesus's example. We must go down deep into the crevices of our souls and deal with the issues, grappling with the pain in our own lives and allowing the Holy Spirit to probe and shed light on areas we have not surrendered to Christ. Before we can be enabled to elevate others, we must deal with the mess in our own lives. Too often we give up on others and ourselves because the mess—in us and them—feels like too much to bear. Nevertheless, through the power of the Holy Spirit and trusting God with all our heart, we permit Him to help us through every difficult place of our life.

God wants us whole and healthy so that we can lead in healthy ways. In the words of David in Psalm 25:10, "All the paths of the LORD are mercy and truth, To such as keep His covenant and His testimonies." Amazing! We too must lead with mercy and truth. Remember that growing and elevating in Christ is an ongoing process of allowing the Holy Spirit to take us from glory to glory, from faith to faith, and from strength to strength. Through the process, God leads us toward greatness, confidence, endurance, and greater stamina to reach new heights in Christ. General Douglas MacArthur once observed, "A true leader has the confidence to stand alone, the courage to make tough decisions, and the compassion to listen to the needs of others. He does not set out to be a leader, but becomes one by the equality of his actions and the integrity of his intent."

Ephesians 4:8–11 gives us a clear picture of five leadership gifts that are vital in developing effective ministry and leadership. Jesus gave the body of Christ **apostles**— men directly commissioned by the Lord to preach the Word and to plant churches in a world that had never had the Gospel preached before. Apostles also who provide foundational impetus so that a work can be sustained. The Apostles' Creed encapsulates the body of truth to which every church must adhere. **Evangelists** are equipped by the Holy Spirit with fire and passion to bring lost souls to Jesus and to stir the body of Christ to win souls. Evangelists also pioneer mission activity, taking the message of salvation to regions beyond, where it has never gone. **Shepherds** nurture and lead the flock to a healthy life in Christ. **Teachers** explain the Scripture in intricate detail and with great anointing and understanding. In addition, Jesus gave us **prophets** to help keep the body on course with what He is doing in the earth. Prophets and prophetic leaders point to God's directions, both corporately and personally. Since Jesus Himself highlighted these leadership roles, the body of Christ should highlight them as well, underscoring when they are visibly obvious in the lives of leaders.

Now let's shift to the seven steps to elevating effective leaders. Jesus gave these gifts of leadership to equip the body of Christ to make disciples and fulfill His great commission. Jesus wants to lift and elevate us so we can be seated with Him in higher places as we lead with love, mercy, and truth.

To elevate means to bring from a lower place to a higher place— to raise. Following the biblical principles from this book will raise the quality of your leadership on multiple levels, assisting you to become a more effective and relevant leader for this time and century. Hold on tight! Get ready to read and learn how to soar in your leadership. I have dedicated more than thirty years to helping people discover their purpose and destiny in Christ Jesus. In my journey God has helped me to refine my purpose, destiny, and leadership quality, and I anticipate that you will benefit in the same way as you immerse yourself in these principles.

Rex Tonkins

MAIN STEPS

Step One: Love
If you lack this quality, you amount to no more than an indecipherable cacophony of noise.

Step Two: Encouragement
Your effectiveness depends on learning how to encourage yourself in the Lord.

Step Three: Attitude
It's all about where you fix (or hang) your thoughts.

Step Four: Delegation
Effective delegating equates to effective discipleship.

Step Five: Endurance
Sustaining enthusiasm empowers your leadership effectiveness.

Step Six: Readiness
Being ready prepares you for divine opportunities.

Step Seven: Servanthood
The foundational quality of a leader is serving.

STEP ONE
LOVE

· · · · · · ·

"Though I speak with the tongues of men and of angels, but have not
love, I have become sounding brass or a clanging cymbal."
(1 Corinthians 13:1)

"Leaders don't force people to follow—they invite
them on a journey." Charles S. Layer

The Scripture says that if we don't have love we amount to no
more than an indecipherable cacophony of noise! The first step
toward effective leadership is leading with love—being concerned,
above our mission and vision, with the well-being of those we lead.
Biblical leadership can be extremely difficult if we try to achieve it
in our own strength. This love about which Paul speaks comes from
our heavenly Father, who is the very author and embodiment of love.
As the Gospel writer points out in John 3:16, "For God so loved the
world that He gave his only begotten Son, that whoever believes in
Him should not perish but have everlasting life."

To love effectively we must have an intimate personal relationship
with Jesus. Further, to love our enemies and those who mistreat
us requires tapping in to this divine, mighty, and infinite love. It
is God alone who gives us the ability to forgive, and it is He who
can take broken things and put them back together again. Love is
surrendering all our hurts to God so that we can work through the
brokenness and find our weakness perfected in His strength. God's
amazing love stretches far enough to help us embrace even those
individuals Satan has used to crush our life. Looking at God's nature

as reflected throughout His Word, we see that He has demonstrated innumerable acts of love and kindness.

God has stipulated that we are to love Him with all our heart, mind, soul, and strength and that His second greatest commandment is to love our neighbor. Love isn't a suggestion but a mandate from heaven. We have to major in love; it's a required course for every person who wants to graduate to the next level. Those who have accepted Jesus as their Lord and Savior and know Him personally understand that loving people is a distinct characteristic of a Christ-follower. If we say we know Christ but do not demonstrate love, we deceive ourselves. There are many leaders across America who claim to love God but refuse to reach across racial, cultural, or denominational lines. Love is all about action and intentionality. Jesus was intentional in reaching out to the Samaritan woman, an individual who represented through ethnicity, religion, and gender a people who were despised by the prevailing culture. When leaders allow God's love to flow through them, God can touch many hearts and minds. Leaders have the ability to either personify God's love or personify Satan's hatred. When we don't allow God's love to flow through us, we are no different from the religious leaders of the time when Jesus walked the earth. It was those religions leaders who crucified Jesus, much as Hitler, driven by hatred, ordered the extermination of the Jewish race.

Still today, the Ku Klux Klan desires to exterminate the black race and despises the Jewish race as well. The Klan, beyond its more overt tactics of hangings, shootings, and arson, has resorted to advocating abortion on demand, working in conjunction with Margaret Sanger, who by founding Planned Parenthood put into motion officially sanctioned genocide. (Documentary called 1939 Birth control review/eugenics.) The Black Panthers, a group formed originally to help protect blacks and citizens from brutality, violence and intimidation, later became a hate organization. Cronyism (the appointment of friends and associates to positions of authority without proper regard to their qualifications) has infiltrated our politics, businesses, and churches by placing people in leadership roles based on the good ol' boy system instead of their qualities and capabilities.

Satan is a master deceiver who drives his agenda through his aversion to all of humankind. Godly leadership understands that Satan perpetuates hatred. Listen to Jesus's own brother on this issue: "If you have bitter envy and self-seeking in your hearts, do not boast and lie against the truth. This ["wisdom"] does not descend from above, but is earthly, sensual, demonic" (James 3:14–15). Satan's objective is to keep animosity alive in our culture, and he has used different mountains of influence to infect our homes with the spirit of hatred. Television, mainstream media, and social media have all become portals for hell and division to infiltrate American homes and enter the hearts and minds of their inhabitants. The sad reality is that we willingly pay for wicked and vile entertainment, marketing, and propaganda to enter our homes—which are intended by God to be places of love, peace, and protection from evil.

God, who loves all people, desires nothing more than for us, His children, to follow suit. If we have a problem with someone else's race, we have a problem with God, who has fearfully and wonderfully created each one of us. God has designed each of us individually as a custom original with intricate and unique abilities. We as His followers are to be conduits of His love, showing His kindness through our acts of caring. God wants His people to personify His love on His earth.

The reality is that many are in pain, grappling with unresolved issues in their homes, schools, businesses, and churches. Many in our culture feel unloved and uncared for—and that includes us as leaders. Let's stop burying our heads in the sand and face the brutal reality that so many of us are hurting. Every leader needs a mentor and accountability partner, someone they can trust implicitly and with whom they can be totally honest and transparent. Having such an individual in our life helps us confess our faults and receive healing. It's only after we have confronted and resolved our own issues that we can be Spirit-empowered to lead by love, to be sensitive to those around us who need the love of God lavished upon them.

I know that I am what I am by God's love, and I am thankful for those leaders who have demonstrated Christ's love to me and helped me through difficult stretches in my life. In the words of another familiar and yet profound quote from John Maxwell, "People don't care how much you know until they know how much you care." Love involves gently correcting wrong behavior and bad attitudes. If a leader can correct you, then God can promote you. God often uses loving leadership to point out obstacles that are hindering our growth. True leadership entails being transparent in terms of our own struggles and shortcomings; it's only then that we can deal with others with humility, knowing how weak we are without God's help.

I remember accepting Christ at the age of twelve and experiencing a degree of love and acceptance I could never before have dreamed possible. God loves and accepts us for who we are, but He doesn't accept the negative behavior we all exhibit at times. The hard truth is that if we choose not to follow God's ways and Word we will suffer the consequences. His love toward us can never change, but the relationship is adversely affected because sin separates us from God. We must daily repent, renounce, and break away from sinful ways—possible only through the enabling power of the Holy Spirit. God disciplines those he loves, but He does so to conform us to the image of Christ.

As I look back over the course of my life, I see clearly those places in which God has disciplined me and corrected my bad attitudes, uncontrolled anger, and sinful actions. God disciplines because He is a loving father who wants the best for us. It is because of His amazing and mighty love that I have dedicated my life to following Jesus. I am profoundly glad to be free of Satan's grip on my life. Satan had me bound in many ways when I was a young adolescent, and his influence continued to impact periods of my adulthood in vulnerable areas of my thinking. Such "strongholds" are beliefs opposite those disseminated through God's Word, thought structures that have been ingrained in us through our upbringing and traumatic experiences. Satan likes to use people to speak the worst over us, causing many of us to give up hope that anything good can come through ourselves.

However, Jesus knew that this young boy, named Rex, needed love, and God used key people in his life to look beyond the behavior to help save him from destruction. These key people have repeatedly shown the love and mercy of God to my life. Andre Crouch used to sing a song that included these lyrics:

> I don't know why Jesus loved me
> I don't know why He cared
> I don't know why He sacrificed His life
> Oh, but I'm glad, so glad He did.

I am profoundly glad that Jesus loved a wretched person like me and made me somebody special. I am writing this book not because I have mastered being a loving leader but because I am connected to the One who has authored and is the Master of love. I understand that I am what I am simply because of His grace. God has helped me accomplish much in my life, education, and athletics, despite my having had parents who were hearing impaired. Despite the communication barrier with parents to whom I couldn't speak with all my heart, God has helped me overcome. Because of Christ in my life, He gave me the discipline to focus and the desire to succeed.

When we know we are loved and cared for we gain a sense of confidence. God has placed special people in my life to care for and support me. He has implanted in every person the ability to give and receive love, along with individuals in each of our lives who can convince and remind us that we are cherished and significant. I give God all the glory for what He has done in my life.

The truth is that rejection can be brutally painful. Rejection is a very difficult problem to deal with, and the situation becomes even harder hitting when one's own family discounts, discards, or outright abandons them. It's normal for a person to want his family in his court of support, but when they're not there for whatever reason it hurts. Satan hurls at us the thought that we are of no value, and if we start believing that lie we'll walk around in despair, assuming that we're rightfully unloved and undeserving of concern. Much of my early bad behavior was based on my seeking love and attention. Even though I now know that I am deeply loved and unconditionally accepted by God, Satan still tries to bring the familiar spirit of rejection into my adulthood, trying to derail me with the same things that derailed me in the past. When this happens I have to remind myself on a regular basis of who I am in Christ.

You and I must keep pressing on toward the goal of our high calling in Christ Jesus. Over the years of my journey with Christ I have experienced great victories and amazing opportunities. Ironically, it has often been during those times that my weaknesses and past issues have seemed to be magnified. Satan attempts to make us forget who we are in Christ, and I have coined a new phrase for the times when he attacks our thinking in this way: D.S.C. (Demonic Spiritual Concussions). Satan tries to hit us hard in what would otherwise be pivotal, productive seasons of our lives in order to get our thinking so warped that we no longer know what we believe and accept doctrines that come from demons. In Paul's words in 1 Timothy 4:1," Now the Spirit expressly says that in latter times some will depart from the faith, giving heed to deceiving spirits and doctrines of demons," When leaders don't tell and preach truth, they become neutered in their conviction of truth, subject to swaying with societal and cultural trends.

Life's challenges and trials reveal that which is deep inside the core of our being. This is why leaders must have a deep reverence for God, to whom each of us must eventually give an account for our decisions. Satan tries to get us to think in ways that will hurt both ourselves and those we influence, and we must continuously be on the alert to avoid this toxic spirit of hate and negative thinking.

When we align our thinking and speaking with the demonic realm, we become our own—and others'—worst enemy. It is imperative that we not become abusive with our words toward family and friends. Too often we align ourselves, perhaps inadvertently, with the kingdom of darkness, using hurtful words and influencing those involved in a situation from a wrong attitude and spirit. There is no justifiable reason for being harsh and unloving to others, whether or not they love us. We as believing fathers and leaders must use the authority given to us by God to bless and not to curse. God is calling us to a right kind of leadership that motivates through loving actions. Healing and refreshing words bring life, but deceitful, vicious words fracture and bruise others' lives.

God gives us a divine order for leading! He jealously—and rightly—insists on being first in our love and loyalty. If we don't have this priority in place, we'll lead in the wrong way, from a self-centered instead of from a God-centered principle of governance, which is the only path to life. When we lead from a self-centered or even from an others-centered mindset, we'll make decisions based on what others say instead of on what God says. Leading from a people-pleaser mentality will get us into trouble with our heavenly Father. When God is first in our allegiance, our leadership will be more effective; loving Him more deeply, we'll follow Him from honest and true motives. We're in dangerous territory when we elevate our family, career, or any other thing or person above God. As Jesus expressed in Matthew 10:37, "He who loves father or mother more than Me is not worthy of Me. And he who loves son or daughter more than Me is not worthy of Me." (NASB)

Loving may sound easy, but it's one of the hardest—and most fundamental—biblical mandates for us to follow, especially in terms of loving our own family when they're unloving toward us. Leaders are responsible to keep on loving despite any lack of love or respect demonstrated by loved ones. We are to stay in the vein of love, and refusing to step down to hate. Hatred and strife are the most opportune portals for Satan to enter a home and relationship. Avoid this way of hate, sticking instead to God's ways of mercy and truth. God is the source of our strength, the anchor of our soul when the storms of life pound against us. Jesus showed us love by going to Calvary to die on the basis of His love for humanity.

Perhaps some have fallen out of love with one another. If so, it's time to elevate ourselves back into love and God's power. Dr. Tony Evans explains the biblical concept of love as passionately and righteously seeking the well-being of another. Biblical love is an act of the will, not fuzzy feelings in the stomach. The entertainment industry has lied to us, trying to convince us that love is a feeling— by its very nature, we know, fickle and fleeting. Jesus clearly tells us that love is action and that biblical love doesn't end.

We can't allow past experiences to erect walls of separation that prevent us from properly loving others. Love puts us in a vulnerable place in which we can be hurt, either intentionally or unintentionally. While I believe that most people don't want to intentionally hurt another person, when we're around people for any length of time misunderstanding and hurt are bound to happen. Our culture has redefined tolerance, positing that just because someone doesn't see from another's viewpoint they're fair game for being called names— that people may legitimately stop loving and disassociate from them. I can tell you that true love doesn't quit or give up on people.

The media and entertainment industry have assisted in putting individuals and families in turmoil; we have allowed the one-eyed monster to dictate our home environment. We allow violence, sex, and profanity to infiltrate our living rooms, to penetrate to the very center of our homes. We have been desensitized and hypnotized, blinded to the effects of Satan's plan to kill, steal, and destroy the image of God embodied in marriage and the family. We bury our heads in the sand as though none of this is happening, but Scripture clearly specifies that words bring both life and death.

I am not pointing the finger at anyone except myself and others who are responsible for guiding their homes in the direction of godliness. Thank God that there are still wholesome movies and entertainment available, and for those individuals who have been raised up to bring healthy, family-centered programming into our homes and hearts. Sadly, portions of the entertainment industry intentionally try to influence the minds of families with wicked ways. God promises that we'll hear from Him when we repent and turn from our wicked ways. The aversion that fills our airways and sound waves comes from the author of hatred, Satan himself. Satan's mode of operation is killing, stealing, and destroying. It's time to elevate ourselves and others above this hateful agenda and align with the frequency of love.

I recall a terrible incident that happened in the late seventies in the city where I was growing up. One early Saturday morning black and white citizens together conducted a rally, declaring "Death to the Klan" in a peaceful demonstration with signs. The unimaginable happened as members of the Ku Klux Klan encroached upon the scene in vans and began opening fire on the protesters. Both black and white people lost their lives on that bleak day in our city's history, smearing a dark stain on the memory of many. Hatred opens a portal for evil to insinuate itself, and it has an alarming propensity to move even otherwise decent people to do dark and wicked things. On that day in 1979 the entire city and region were in a state of deep shock, with citizens of all races, ages, and socio-economic levels deeply saddened by the carnage. Living only minutes away from the scene of this heinous act, I wondered why and how this could have happened in a friendly city like ours. Shortly afterward I stepped outside on an overcast day, looking up to heaven and asking the question "Why can't we love one another?" Decades later I still ask the same question. Back in the seventies as a young adolescent I made the decision that I would choose love and rise above hate and racism.

It's only through the love of God that people can indiscriminately love others. God has placed within my heart His own love for human souls, no matter their race, creed, or culture. Godly leaders must be filled with love and led by the Holy Spirit to demonstrate God's love. And they must lead with a balance of mercy and justice. In the words of David in Psalm 101:1, "I will sing of mercy and justice; To You, O LORD, I will sing praises." Allow your life to sing out to all people that you love them and want justice for them.

The day I married Vickie in 1987 my pastor spoke over us the familiar and beloved words of 1 Corinthians 13:13: "And now abide faith, hope, and love, these three; but the greatest of these is love." He pointed out that there would be days when our trust would ebb but that we were to keep the faith in God. He also alerted us that there would be days when our hope would wane and we wouldn't feel like loving each other but that we were to keep on hoping and loving. How right he was to remind us that though feelings are as fickle as the weather we were to remember the covenant we had made before a holy God who holds us accountable for our attitudes and actions. When we're filled with the love of God we're more inclined to love and forgive our mate. *Love* is a verb that continues to show itself through acts of kindness. Love is a commitment lived out.

I am dedicating this chapter on love to the leaders who have loved me regardless of my ways. Truth be told, I don't know where I would be if these leaders hadn't shown me the love I needed. I'm thankful to my pastor for correcting my actions when I fired all the volunteers for not being in place when we were preparing for a big weekend youth outreach event. Every one of those volunteers was hurt by the way I handled the situation, and my pastor talked to me about this not being the way to handle people. We called a special meeting with all the leaders of the youth ministry, at which I apologized for my actions. Proverbs 12:1 couldn't be clearer: "Whoever loves instruction loves knowledge, But he who hates correction is stupid."

My pastor helped me develop discipline and understanding so I could grow and become a better leader. Unfortunately, some of those youth leaders felt as though they could no longer trust my leadership and decided not to continue helping in the youth ministry. One pays a heavy price for leading from the impetus of anger. I asked them to come back and serve, but many were still hurt and irate. My pastor informed me that while he understood why I had done what I did, I couldn't in the future handle a situation that way just because I was upset. He invited me to talk to him first if I felt tempted to react in this way.

This leader took the time to love me and show me how things should be done. The process didn't feel good but was vital for my maturity as a leader. When the time came around for our weekly youth service we found ourselves with a roomful of youth but an insufficient ratio of leaders to students to sufficiently serve these rambunctious adolescents. Thank the Lord that Chris and Nadine— two of the volunteer leaders I had "fired" and "rehired"—showed up to help us assist. These dedicated leaders chose to forgive my actions and get back to the business of serving our youth. That day taught me the power of forgiveness and humility, and I was thrilled to see them. Since that time I have personally witnessed God elevating their leadership to amazing heights, enabling them to soar as eagles for His glory. To this day I remain thankful for this godly couple and their friendship. They gave me a divine boost that day back in the nineties—one I will never forget.

The thing that amazes me about the Lord is how He uses our failures and mistakes as lessons to advance His kingdom. As Paul reminds us is Romans 8:28, "We know that all things work together for good to those who love God, to those who are called according to His purpose." God is amazingly merciful to use and love us even after we've made a mess of things. I definitely don't deserve His mercy and graciousness toward me. Jesus said that if we love Him we will obey Him. We have to first submit to God's will and way before He can elevate our leadership to the point that it will reflect His nature. It's imperative for leaders to grow in wisdom throughout their leadership journey. In the words of Proverbs 19:8, "He who gets wisdom loves his own soul; He who keeps understanding will find good." Leaders must continuously be moving toward learning that will improve and elevate their leadership.

In Hosea 4:6 God pronounces the sad verdict that "my people are destroyed for lack of knowledge." This speaks to me of our need to continue in our desire to gain knowledge. In order to do so, leaders must devote themselves to prayer and the study of Scripture. Effective leaders are readers—with God's Word their priority in terms of source material. It's time to elevate and stop allowing Satan to outsmart us because we lack the discernment, knowledge, and wisdom to identify and expose error. God's Word tells us to be vigilant and alert to Satan schemes. The devil's intent is to deceive us and to destroy our destiny, leaving us in utter ruin. We're called to put on our armor daily and to keep ourselves filled with the Holy Spirit, so that when our leadership is challenged our adversaries will pull from our lives the fruit of the Spirit: love, joy, peace, longsuffering, gentleness, goodness, meekness, faith, and self-control. Paul enjoins us in Philippians 2:2–3 to "fulfill my joy being like-minded, having the same love, being of one accord, of one mind. Let nothing be done through selfish ambition or conceit, but in lowliness of mind let each esteem others better than himself."

Love is a distinct mark in all arenas of effective leadership. As Vince Lombardi declared, "You've got to care for one another. You have to love each other. Most people call it team spirit." Jesus gives a solid picture of what love looks like in His high definition of the term in Luke 10:25–37:

> Behold, a certain lawyer stood up and tested Him, saying, "Teacher, what shall I do to inherit eternal life?" He said to him, "What is written in the law? What is your reading of it?" So he answered and said, "'You shall love the Lord your God with all your heart, with all your soul, with all your strength, and with all your mind,' and 'your neighbor as yourself.'" And He said to him, "You have answered rightly; do this and you will live." But he, wanting to justify himself, said to Jesus, "And who is my neighbor?" Then Jesus answered and said: "A certain man went down from Jerusalem to Jericho, and fell among thieves, who stripped him of his clothing, wounded him, and departed, leaving him half dead. Now by chance a certain priest came down that road. And when he saw him, he passed by on the other side. Likewise, a Levite, when he arrived at the place, came and looked, and passed by on the other side. But a certain Samaritan, as he journeyed, came where he was. And when he saw him, he had compassion. So he went to him and bandaged his wounds, pouring on oil

and wine; and he set him on his own animal, brought him to an inn, and took care of him. On the next day, when he departed, he took out two denarii, gave them to the innkeeper, and said to him, 'Take care of him; and whatever more you spend, when I come again, I will repay you.' So which of these three do you think was neighbor to him who fell among the thieves?" And he said, "He who showed mercy on him." Then Jesus said to him, "Go and do likewise."

I like to share an amazing story involving my son, Christian, and my daughter, Victoria. When we were in North Carolina we rented a house from my cousin for six months while having a home built. Our son Christian demonstrated love by taking care of his sister in an emergency fire situation.

Christian's memory of that day:

> It was a snow day so we had no school. Mom and Dad gave us a list of chores to do. One was to do laundry. I put the towels in the laundry and did the rest of the chores. I put those towels in the dryer later on. As we were finishing up, I started smelling smoke. I couldn't figure out where it was coming from. I almost dismissed the smoke smell. Then I looked at the dryer and saw smoke coming from it. I opened the dryer and the towels were on fire. I looked frantically for a fire extinguisher and couldn't find one. I then got a big bowl and began throwing water on the fire. I yelled for my sister to go out to the front of the house and call Mom and Dad. I then ran outside and grabbed a water hose and put the fire out with that. I opened all the doors to air out the house and waited in the front till the fire department got there.

Victoria's memory:

> Christian was doing laundry and went to go check on it. We were watching a movie and then he called me kind of frantically. I just said, "What?" No answer. Then I said "what?" again, and heard nothing. I ran to see what was wrong, and he said, "There is a fire." Christian told me to get back and call Mom and Dad. I immediately called them and then my dad called the fire department. My brother put out the fire and we sat on the front porch until everyone arrived. When the fire department arrived, they were surprised that Christian had put the

fire out. They said that on school days when children are home alone they receive many calls, but some don't turn out so well.

Even though school was cancelled that day, Christian still had a varsity basketball game against rival Page Pirates. Christian still had the smell of smoke in his pores, and that put a fire of intensity into his game where he played with an unstoppable force, scoring 17 points. The point of this story is that Christian's first thought was to protect his sister. His actions demonstrated a special love he has had for his sister from the day she was born.

Elevate Leadership Point:

Coach Woodward cared enough to hold me accountable for my academic progress—precisely the kind of love in action I needed in high school. We had to report to the gymnasium to show him our grades, and the two teammates in front of me were immediately sent back to the education wing based on grades he didn't like or approve. When he looked at mine I was understandably nervous, wondering whether I would get the same response as the others. Instead, Coach Woodward said something astounding: "Rex, you are smart."

I responded with an incredulous "I am?" His words infused me with destiny, confidence, and the motivation to improve academically. Coach empowered me to think differently about myself, my educational pursuits, and my life. He changed the way I viewed myself and helped me strive for greater academic and athletic excellence. This is what real and effective, elevating leadership is all about. I recently received a letter from my old high school coach. Coach Woodward stated, "Coach Rex, I am so proud of you and your work with the Destiny Project. You have certainly been a source of inspiration to Mrs. Woodward and me. May God continue to bless the Tonkins family and the work of Destiny. Sincerely, Coach." These words, even so many years after our athlete/coach relationship, are priceless in their encouragement.

To operate effectively, leaders must be about encouraging, empowering, equipping, and helping those they lead to excel. We are infinitely important to God, though too often we gauge our significance and value by measuring ourselves against unrealistic worldly standards. God established our value before our conception, fashioning each of us as a masterpiece with unique abilities and attributes—to the point that our laughter is distinct and even our fingerprint patterns exclusive. These delightful distinctions among persons personify His love for infinite variety. Satan is continuously at work to deceive us into thinking we are of no worth, but God directs us not to reject that which He Himself has accepted and values. To close out this chapter I want to take a look at what Scripture specifies about love. According to 1 Corinthians 13:4–7, love

1. suffers long,
2. is kind,
3. doesn't envy or
4. parade itself,
5. isn't puffed up,
6. doesn't behave rudely,
7. doesn't seek its own,
8. isn't easily provoked,
9. keeps no record of being wronged,
10. doesn't rejoice in iniquity
11. but rejoices in the truth,
12. bears all things,
13. believes all things,
14. hopes all things, and
15. endures all things.

Anne Graham Lotz, the daughter of Dr. Billy Graham, observes that "the first secret to loving others is to immerse yourself in a love relationship with God the Father, God the Son, and God the Holy Spirit and abide there." We as leaders must endeavor to abide in God's presence if we're to abide in His divine, mighty love for others.

Billy Graham also says," I am convinced the greatest act of love we can ever perform for people is to tell them about God's love for them in Christ."

Closing:

Allow me to observe that love is worth fighting for, that it's embodied in action, and that we don't have to look very far to realize that Satan has initiated an all-out assault to destroy the family values that have helped forge America. It's time for us as Christian leaders to wake up because none of us is exempt from demonic attacks that can completely damage an individual life or that of a family. It's time for us to yield to God's way.

In the words of Butch Lee,

> Love is the foundational element of leadership; from the time we accept Christ as our Savior and Lord our views, attitudes, and thoughts are being continually reformatted by and conformed to the Word of God and to the manner in which Christ responds to the issues of life. If you allow the process to unfold unimpeded, everything with which you are faced will be run through the filter of love. There is no divine guarantee that this will be an easy walk, nor will your decisions necessarily come without angst. It does mean that you will have a God-based filter to help you in the process of being a leader.

The Old Testament leader Nehemiah reports, "I looked, and arose and said to the nobles, to the leaders, and to the rest of the people, 'Do not be afraid of them. Remember the Lord, great and awesome, and fight for your brethren, your sons, your daughters, your wives, and your houses" (Nehemiah 4:14). The verb form used here for "looked" (Hebrew *ra'ah*) implies "perceived." Men and women of God, fight on your knees in prayer for your families and for those others you lead and about whom you care, and take action on the instructions God speaks to you. Keep standing in faith, keep hoping, and keep loving, for at the end of your life you'll realize that what is most important is relationship, no matter how hard it may have been at times to overcome evil with good. When you draw your last breath, ready at last to be ushered in to the peace of Jesus, you will know that you have done all you could to love and assist others. According to Scripture, from heaven's perspective love settles it all.

Elevate Facts:

Faith in God's ability helps us to love.
Acquiring the fruits of the Spirit is vitally important in leading.
Christ in you constitutes your hope of glory.
Tough love is still love.

Seven L's of Love:

1. Live a life that demonstrates love.
2. Lifestyle for you as a leader must be all about demonstrating loving acts of kindness.
3. Leave a legacy of love for your children to follow.
4. Learn to love unconditionally like your Father.

5. Lead in your love and in your actions.
6. Learn to love more.
7. Listening is an action of love.

Elevate Questions:

1. Why is love so vitally important for you as a leader?
2. What are the characteristics of love?
3. Why is it that accountability and love go hand in hand? How did Coach Woodward show tough love to Rex?
4. How can you overcome hate and evil? (Check out Romans 12:21.)
5. What is God's divine order in terms of leadership priorities? Rate the following in their proper sequence of importance: self-orientation, God-orientation, and others-orientation.
6. According to James 3:14–15, what characteristics are revealed when hatred rather than love is operative in a situation?
7. How do you love God with all your heart, mind, soul, and strength? Be as specific as possible.

Leaders' Prayer:

Jesus stated in John 13:34–35, "A new commandment I give to you, that you love one another; as I have loved you, that you also love one another. By this all will know that you are My disciples, if you have love for one another." Father, help us to demonstrate this biblical mandate to love one another, so that people may clearly see and know that we are your disciples. In Jesus's name, Amen.

STEP TWO
ENCOURAGEMENT

• • • • • • •

> "Now David was greatly distressed, for the people
> spoke of stoning him, because the soul of all the
> people was grieved, every man for his sons and his
> daughters. But David strengthened himself in the
> LORD his God." (1 Samuel 30:6)

> "To be able to lead others, a man must be willing to
> go forward alone." Harry Truman

Encourage is a verb implying the giving of support, confidence, or hope to someone else—emboldening, strengthening, or helping them. We as leaders may miss the importance of encouraging *ourselves* in difficult moments, however. David discovered the key in his leadership journey for overcoming major problems: inquiring of God.

The Lord has the solution to every problem we'll ever face. We must go to the Father in prayer, communing (communicating intimately) with Him, developing a consistent prayer life that will enable us to listen to the whispers of God's solution to the problem at hand. Life can deal us seemingly insurmountable blows, but God will guide and help us, showing us the path to victory, as He did with David.

A particularly thorny issue can involve those closest to us for whatever reason standing against us. David's men were ready to stone him because of what had happened to their families. In difficult times we need friends and family to stand with us; unfortunately, as every leader knows so well, this doesn't always happen. It can be agonizing

17

for leaders when their friends or family members are ready to throw them under the bus.

Scripture clearly explains how things will be in the last days. As leaders, we must make it our goal and focus to be led by the Holy Spirit. Satan's goal and agenda are to kill, steal, and destroy anything that reflects and magnifies the Lord, so no matter the circumstances leaders must make it a practice to go to the Father for strength, consolation, and resolution. David discovered that when he inquired of the Lord he found courage and even strategy. Aligning with God's way and plan helped David and his men overcome to the point of recovering their abducted families and belongings. We must remember that God knows what is best and that He reveals the strategies of success. God's Word shows us how to keep our marriage, family, and testimony unspotted. This is why it's imperative for leaders to daily inquire of the Lord to gain personal and corporate victory in their lives. To be an effective leader one must have a spiritual ear to detect the whispers of God's daily, divine instructions, especially in moments of crisis. We all need God and others in our life to support us.

To share a personal example, I was in training in Greensboro, North Carolina, to become a firefighter. The facility was a class-one station with top national ratings, and my training got off to a great start. I was appointed by our chiefs and captain as a class captain and had excellent rapport with the chief. Leadership isn't always popular, however, especially when others don't listen to directives. As a captain in this class I wanted to listen and learn all I could while be respectful to authority. In our class sessions we were instructed by the leaders to sit quietly.

Our particular class of about forty members included retired highway patrolman and military veterans who were making the fire department a second career. The predicament for the newbies was that these older, seasoned leaders knew the protocols but refused to follow them, wanting everyone else to follow suit. While others were talking and joking I sat quietly at the very front of the classroom. All I could think about was the prospect of the chief entering the classroom and hearing all the commotion . . . and the rest of us running additional miles for failing to follow a clear directive. One of the retired leaders, a former military a drill sergeant, commented, "Tonkins, I don't see and hear you laughing."

I turned around and stated, "We were told to sit quietly, and I don't hear anything funny."

There were sounds of Ahhh! and Oohh! before everyone fell quiet. Minutes later the superiors came in. Allow me to clarify that my motive to be a firefighter was something other than a passion for fighting fires. The opportunity, in my mind, would afford me a convenient and flexible venue to do what I love: teaching and training youth. God's Word points out in Proverbs 16:9 that though we make our plans God has the final say. In the meantime, I was making great strides in the classroom and in the field of training.

However, one weekend in October I didn't get ample study time due to my hosting and facilitating a youth outreach and accommodating a guest youth group from Atlanta, Georgia, which required much of my time and focus over the weekend. So when Monday arrived I was less than prepared for our weekly exam. A requirement for firefighters was to pass all exams, though a recruit was allowed to retake two exams with grades below seventy points. Retaking the failed exam required doubling up on study time and effort, reviewing the previous week's information while staying current with the new material. I did a retake and passed, while feeling the pressure to keep up with all the new information.

As we moved forward, the training and new material were becoming more intense and difficult. December arrived, and we reached the pinnacle of our training, which involved preparing for our final exam in order to advance and graduate as certified firefighters. I successfully passed the exams until we reached the final one. The weekend before that test I studied relentlessly in our small apartment, trying to connect with study groups to ensure that I had the bases successfully covered. When I went to bed on Saturday night, however, I had a vivid and detailed dream of failing the exam—of scoring a sixty-five, a five-point deficit. The dream included my turning in my exam and one of the leaders summoning me to go and see the chief. Upon my arrival in the chief's office he revealed my less than stellar score. As I write about this, I still feel the pain of the experience.

I awoke in great anxiety and attempted to assure myself that this dream wasn't of God. However, I couldn't put it out of my mind and studied into the late hours on Sunday. Monday morning arrived, and I worked on the 8:00 a.m. test for four hours before finally turning it in to one of the captains. A few moments went by as I waited for the results. Just as in the dream, a captain came out and escorted me to the chief's office—and just as in the dream my score was revealed to be a sixty-five. Obviously, mine had been a prophetic dream to prepare me because my plans, employment status, and financial prospects had just changed. The chief commented that he found the results hard to understand; I had been one of the best leaders, and the only conceivable explanation in his mind was that God must have something more important for me to do.

In the words of Chuck Swindoll, "Life is ten percent of what happens to you and ninety percent your response." We all make the choice each day either to get better or to get bitter. I arrived home, changed clothes, and began to sing praises to the Lord. Not surprisingly, it was during this time in His presence that I found strength. I also wept before the Lord for hours, broken and embarrassed. I had devoted considerable effort, energy, and sacrifice to this endeavor and had come up short by a measly five points. Not only was Vickie pregnant with Victoria and our son only four years old, but we now had no medical insurance.

God gave me strength the next day to go to His house and work on youth ministry projects. As I trudged down the long hallway that was nicely polished with a fresh coat of wax, I approached the door to the pastor's office, intending to pass by. He unexpectedly opened it, however, stepped out, and greeted me with obvious joy, asking how I was doing. Pausing for a moment, I stated humbly, "I didn't make it as firefighter." His response: "Ah! I am sorry." Then seemingly out of nowhere his expression lit up, and he declared, "You are the man! You are the man!" These same words had been spoken when I was in high school and my coach had appointed me captain of the track team.

Obviously bewildered and wondering what the pastor might have had in mind, I waited for his explanation. He informed me that those involved in a meeting that had just wrapped up had been praying about the need for a director to help launch the Malachi House, a home for men with life-controlling problems. I immediately dismissed his suggestion with thoughts of *Not me. I'm the youth guy. I don't have and never have had drugs or alcohol problems*. He asked me to pray about the offer and talk to Vickie. This prospect was totally unrelated to my plans, but God's ways and thoughts are infinitely higher than our own. His doors seldom look like the ones we envision.

I didn't want to go this route of helping men with substance-abuse problems. I was convinced that I was not qualified. What I failed to take into account is that God qualifies those He calls. Moses didn't feel adequate for leading the children of Israel out of bondage, but God used him as he willingly yielded to His will and plan. After Vickie and I had prayed and discussed the Malachi House job, we agreed to this divine assignment with a salary of only eight hundred dollars a month. The fire training had been a good experience, and I had learned a lot about practical leadership, but the Malachi House experience would train me to lead with divine leadership; I would have to rely totally on God in dealing with men who were much older than myself and had years of experience in lying and manipulating to get their way. As things turned out, the training through which God would take me would propel me forward to places I could never have imagined—and all because of intimate prayer, inquiring of the Lord, and following divine guidance. Throughout the years since that experience God has helped me place my trust in Him as the source for all my needs.

Leading the Malachi House helped me see how vital encouragement is to people. Research reveals that it takes twelve positive impressions to overcome a negative one. To lead effectively we must lead from a pure heart, clean conscience, and sincere faith (1 Timothy 1:5). Leaders must be encouragers because people all around us feel defeated and discouraged. A word of encouragement, in fact, can shift a person's entire destiny. Just as when my coach and pastor had announced "You are the man!" God assured me that He Himself had chosen me, had given me a future and a hope (see Jeremiah 29:11). If you're going through a trial and are ready to quit, I say to you *be encouraged in the Lord!* Leaders must continually look for ways to encourage those around them. In the words of Proverbs 27:17, "As iron sharpens iron, So a man sharpens the countenance of his friend." We all need a friend who will listen and help us see a bright future in the light of Christ. Let our words be that of encouragement to everyone we meet (Ephesians 4:29). Remember that Jesus is the way, the truth, and the life. When we yield to God's ways and follow God's truth we will experience a life that encourages others to follow suit. As we sharpen our life in God we help sharpen others as well.

Elevate Leadership Moment:

I recall my tenth-grade year in high school, when I had just finished a fantastic football season injury free. After the season was over some of my teammates and neighborhood friends wanted to play sandlot football, with no pads or equipment. On one particular play I was running the football when one of the veteran players grabbed my shirt and swung me around, causing me to lose my balance and crash, shoulder first, into the cold, muddy, and hard surface. Participants around me heard the loud pop of my collarbone breaking. As I attempted to lift up my shoulder it fell over, limp. Another setback in this young football player's career.

I began trudging home, unaccompanied, as my teammates and the area players kept right on playing. As I began the slow descent to my house, a little less than a mile away, I had to brace my shoulder against my body and use my other hand to hold the broken collarbone. When I finally arrived no one was home, so I waited outdoors until someone else came. My brother Isaac finally drove me to Moses Cone Hospital for medical care. As painful as the experience was, I was encouraged by the quality of my mother's care. It was necessary for her to assist me for weeks just to sit up and get out of bed. The pain was excruciating, but she gave me the push I needed each morning. Still to this day, I thank God for my mom, without whose help I don't know how I would have made it.

It's almost as though the Lord Himself gives us that push, that encouragement and support, when we need it. Three years later, in 1984, I was preparing and packing up my 1968 Volkswagen bug to head off to college. I will never forget seeing my dad tear up at the prospect. At that moment I realized for the first time that he deeply loved me. Sadly, I had often surmised that my dad didn't love me because he had taken a pass on disciplining me, even though I knew I needed it. My heart was encouraged in my knowledge of his love and care as I drove up to Lee Street and headed to I-40 to travel west to Cullowhee, North Carolina.

These two events helped me see a healthy side of my parents that greatly encouraged my heart. Looking back, I realized that they cared about each other and appreciated the fact that I was learning to be independent and do things of my own initiative without getting into lots of trouble, as had been my custom during my earlier years. Salvation in Christ had taught me to cooperate with leaders and teachers and to develop a sense of harmony with others and myself.

The experience of a single season at Western Carolina University taught this inner-city boy some lifetime wisdom. I knew that I would have to align with God's plan if I were to succeed—and that if I remained at Western another semester I would dry up spiritually and be less likely to further my education. I made the difficult decision not to return. During my final semester of high school the year before, God in His infinite mercy had sent a recruiting coach named Shuler from Lenoir Rhyne University. Now, following that single semester at Western Carolina University, Coach Shuler visited our home on Dillard Street and gave me a second opportunity to enter the place I had originally planned to attend. Amazingly, I found myself in school at Lenoir Rhyne that same day.

Upon my arrival I immediately made friends who were involved with the Fellowship of Christian Athletes. My new friends loved God, and we encouraged one another in the faith. Even when at times it was uncomfortable to be truthful and transparent, this mutual encouragement helped us mature in the faith at a rapid pace. I remember riding with my friend John in his Mercury Lynx, headed west on the campus, when a car unexpectedly backed into our path, with John unable to avoid striking it on its side. Soon enough came the moment of truth! When the police officer arrived on the scene his first question was "Did you all have on seat belts?" Unfortunately, for us back in 1985 the seat belt law had just come into effect. Glancing at one another, John and I could see Christ in each other and knew we had to tell the truth: "Officer, we didn't have on seat belts." Since we told the truth, we assumed he would just give us a warning. Not! We were both slapped with twenty-five dollar tickets. For us as college students twenty-five dollars was a lot of money.

John Quincy Adams once said, "If your actions inspire others to dream more, do more and become more, you are a leader." John and I were both progressing in the direction of leadership, as evidenced by our inspiration to do the right thing. The leader's primary role is simply to encourage with words, promote and empower people who are faithful, and equip others with practical tools so they can be successful in their endeavors. My friend John Bornschein, a pastor in Colorado Springs, observed that a leader continually motivates people to reach toward high goals. In essence, leaders are cheerleaders.

Elevate Leadership Moment:

We were playing the eleventh-ranked team in the nation, with All-Americans on the team. This team was a high favorite to beat us by several touchdowns. As the game began, however, the Lenoir Rhyne Bears rose to our opponent's level of play. Our defense did an amazing job of clamping down the Presbyterian offense, giving us the opportunity to execute our game plan. We also had an All-American receiver, Terrence Stewart, who was double and triple covered by the Presbyterian defense. Our offensive backfield, the running backs, had passing route assignments to draw defenders away from our All-American receiver. As the plays were called, my assignment was to run a passing route straight down the field, with the goal of pulling the free safety away from our number-one receiver.

Immediately noticing that the Presbyterian defenders had all eyes on Terrence, the All-American suggested that they might literally let me go down the field uncovered. I returned to the huddle and told the quarterback I was wide open, and we executed the exact play we had planned, with the exception that Brian, our quarterback, would actually pass the ball to me. As our quarterback sounded off the cadence down—*set, hut, hut*—the center snapped the ball before taking a few steps back. I took off in a sprint down the field near the hash marks in the middle. Once again the safety shifted toward Terrence, allowing me to proceed downfield uncovered. I caught the eyes of our quarterback and watched him launch the ball high into the air. I reached up, running in a full stride, and caught the football for a touchdown, entering the end zone unchallenged. My thirty- to forty-yard touchdown evened the score seven to seven. We went into halftime tied, frustrating the Presbyterian team.

In the second half the Presbyterian offense scored quickly, marching downfield at will and making the score 21–14. Our offense sputtered, and we went three downs and out. I recall moments in the game when the players from the Presbyterian defense hit very hard, making it difficult for us to run the ball and pass it. The Presbyterian team played dirty, too, meaning that they tried to hurt players and made illegal hits the referees couldn't see. In the pile stuff happens; once tackled, a player may be poked in the eye, hit, or have his ankles twisted. I began to get frustrated; not only was I being hit hard, but I was also being poked and hit after the whistle to stop play had been blown. I asked the official whether he could see what the players were doing after the play, but he offered no response. My recourse was turning to God—yes, even there on the football field. I asked, "Lord, do you see what they're doing to your son?"

From that moment the momentum of the game began to shift in our favor. We were able to start moving the ball and get some first downs. However, we didn't score on that particular series and had to punt the ball back to Presbyterian. Then came the big break! When we punted, one of our players ran downfield as fast as he could and got a solid hit on the punt returner, causing a fumble. We were pumped at getting the ball back, within good field position. The score remained 21–14, Presbyterian, with time winding down. Our coach noticed that we were able to run the football, and I carried the ball back to back, moving closer to the goal. As we neared the goal line we had a first and goal less than five yards from it. We ran isolation left, crossing the line, but the official determined that we were short a foot. Second down, with every ounce of strength and effort again isolation right—but the official said no. Third down and goal, run isolation again. I made sure to cross the line of scrimmage, but the official said no yet again. I looked in amazement at the ball, now clearly in the end zone.

Our coach called time out as we proceeded to the sideline; out of breath and in pain, I announced, "Coach, you may want to get somebody else in." Coach declined, directing me to stay in there and get that ball into the end zone. As we returned to the line of scrimmage, I remember thinking, *I* will *get into the end zone, and I'm going to leap so high it will be very clear that I've made a touchdown*. As we called my number, again isolation left, I ran and jumped as high as I possibly could, leaping over the oncoming defenders and scoring the touchdown with only three seconds left on the clock: score 21–20. We called time out again to decide whether we wanted to kick the extra point to tie the game and go into overtime or score two points with a run or pass play. Our coach instructed us to run the exact same play, with one slight change: our quarterback was to fake the ball to me but keep it; this was called a bootleg play. We would have to put on the best acting performance of our football career.

The quarterback was ready—*set, hut*—and our offensive line, consisting of tight end Rex Harris, tackle Ron Lundy, guard Eric Brandon, center Carson Gown, guard Kevin Hunt, and tackle Kyle Patterson, all came off the line with force as though we were running the identical play in which we had just scored a touchdown. I ran and leaped even harder, pretending to have received the football. As intended, the entire defense converged on me. With amazing execution our quarterback, Brian, had faked the ball to me but kept it. Running opposite the fake, he circled around toward the right and literally ran into the end zone untouched, scoring the two-point conversion with no time remaining on the clock.

The score now 21–22, we won the game in dramatic fashion. As the defenders gazed at me in bafflement, I pointed at our quarterback. To this very day, whenever I think of that game I get a smile on my face reflecting on what I consider to have been a great moment in history. Truly, God hears and cares about the things that concern us. Leaders, no matter how badly the odds may seem to be stacked against you, keep on fighting for your loved ones, as God has called you to do. As Anne Graham Lotz once counseled, "Don't concentrate on what you lack, concentrate on what you have. Then give all of it to Jesus for His use."

I want to encourage you to be confident and to walk in victory, because Jesus has given us the victory and made us to be more than conquerors. Too often people allow their circumstances to dictate their attitude and trajectory. I challenge you to seek God as you've never done before and discover the glorious richness of your purpose and destiny in Christ.

In 1 Corinthians 16:13–14 the apostle Paul exhorts each of us to "Watch, stand fast in the faith, be brave, be strong. Let all that you do be done with love." Decide to encourage yourself in the Lord, and you'll be empowered to encourage others who need it. In essence, leaders are cheerleaders, cheering people on in their journey of faith. My friend Brian Dalen shared with me his own leadership story, including these preliminary observations:

> Looking back over my twenty-year engineering career, I have had great leaders over me. Those who had the greatest impact on me were those who had a desire to see me get better and thrive at my job, versus seeing themselves elevated or getting a promotion. Someone once told me to give myself away in my job by equipping those under me with everything I know. Don't keep it to yourself, for job security or self-edification, but give it away. This is a principle of God, and you'll always find that you cannot out-give Him. When you give away your wisdom and knowledge, somehow you'll be given even more wisdom and knowledge. This is a win/win for the receiver and the giver.

Brian went on:

> In 1982, when I was eighteen, I headed off to Hickory, North Carolina, from Green Cove Springs, Florida, to attend Lenoir Rhyne University on a football scholarship. The football team always arrived two weeks early, before school started, to begin practices. This was the first time I had been away from home, and I was very homesick. When my roommate quit during the first week of practice and returned home, I was by myself and wondering if this was for me. Soon afterward I decided to pack my bags and return to Florida, never wishing to return to Lenoir Rhyne. When I returned home I worked odd jobs and was planning to pursue a walking-on opportunity with a community college baseball team. Before committing to pursue the community college option, I received a call from the recruiting coach from

Lenoir Rhyne, asking if I would be interested in coming back in January and going through spring drills with the team. At first I was reluctant, but he said to think about it and he would call me back. I prayed to God daily, asking for guidance, and on the day the coach called back I had peace from God to say yes.

When January rolled around and I was driving to North Carolina, I was praying to God every mile of the trip. I asked God for one friend who could help me make it through. When I arrived at Lenoir Rhyne University I was assigned a roommate, David Moose, whom I got along with immediately. David was a transfer from the University of North Carolina Tar Heels football team. He had been an incredible football standout in high school and college, receiving many accolades as an athlete and a scholar. He did not slow down when he got to Lenoir Rhyne and was named the captain of the football team at the end of our first year, while making straight A's in the classroom. One of the reasons David immediately rose to a leadership position on our football team was his desire to encourage the younger players, including myself. After our practices were over and we were back in the dorm room at night, it was always packed with players aspiring to be like David. We liked David because he gave us his time and attention and genuinely cared about our interest and well-being. He didn't speak down to us but imparted his wisdom about football, discipline on and off the field, and developing a good attitude, not only through words but by example.

"God answered my prayers," declares Brian, "through divine appointment connecting me with David Moose. David's leadership helped me get through that first year in college and helped me to become a leader who would eventually help others."

Elevate Facts:

Fight for what is rightfully yours. God has given you the victory!
Accept instructions from the Lord in how to win the victory!
Courage—ask God for the courage to do whatever He shows you.
Trust God despite what you see with your natural eye!

The Seven E's of Encouragement:

1. Equip yourself to encourage.
2. Evaluate yourself regarding how you are encouraging others.
3. Empower people with words of life.
4. Enjoy people.
5. Experience what it means to be a true friend.
6. Encapsulate moments to help others excel.
7. Endeavor to keep the unity of the Spirit.

Elevate Questions:

1. Why is it vitally important for us as leaders to learn to encourage ourselves in the Lord?
2. In what ways has your family been vital when you've experienced setbacks?
3. Why should friends help each other do what is right? (See Micah 6:8.)
4. What was the key turning point in the game against Presbyterian?
5. Why is seeking divine assistance vital in leading?
6. How was God's mercy displayed toward Rex?
7. Why is it important that leaders become encouragers and cheerleaders? (See Romans 15:13.)

Leaders' Prayer:

Father, help us endeavor to seek you so that we'll be infused with encouragement to carry out your agenda in relation to the discouraged, and help us live in harmony as brothers and sisters. In Jesus's name, Amen.

STEP THREE
ATTITUDE

· · · · · · ·

"Finally, brethren, whatever things are true,
whatever things are noble, whatever things are just,
whatever things are pure, whatever things
are lovely, whatever things are of good report,
if there is any virtue and if there is anything
praiseworthy—meditate on these things. The things
which you learned and received and heard and saw
in me, these do, and the God of peace will be with
you." (Philippians 4:8–9)

"A highly credible leader under-promises and over
delivers." John Maxwell

My friend Darryl from Chesapeake, Virginia, with whom I had the privilege of coaching basketball in Colorado Springs, went into the archives and shared this detailed memory of a coaching moment that changed the way we approached our position and has helped us look at every opponent with a different mindset. He titled this story "Karval Cornbread Fed":

> The varsity men's basketball team was on a roll, winning back-to-back games against two conference foes and positioning the Jaguars atop their conference, all alone in first place. Next up for the conference-leading Jaguars were the junior and senior high school Trojans from ninety miles east of Colorado Springs. Karval was a small farming community with a population of about two hundred fifty residents. The local school was

a combined middle and senior high school with fewer than ninety students. As we loaded up the van to travel to Karval for the game, many of the players began to ask where and how far away our destination was. Long before the days of the mobile GPS, the good old road atlas showed the players the location of the small farming town. As I slowly pointed my index finger in its direction, the players began to raise their eyebrows in dismay. "Boondocks," shouted one player; "Sticks," exclaimed another. We all laughed as we loaded the van, fully confident that this would be an easy, routine win on the road. Typically before a game, Coach Rex and I would ensure that the players were mentally prepared. We would urge each player to think about what we wanted to accomplish during the game. A normal practice was for the forwards and center to set a goal of how many rebounds they wanted to get, and the guards set similar goals.

As we set out on I-94 heading west toward Karval, the pregame ritual deviated from the norm in that no one thought about goals or began to prepare themselves mentally. Instead, everyone, including the coaching staff, enjoyed the pregame banter, laughing and joking with one another. About an hour into the ride many of the players noticed that we were no longer in the well-manicured suburbs of Colorado Springs but were riding past farm after sprawling farm. Seeing the fields fueled everyone's confidence, and the players were feeling bold. "Cornbread Fed! Cornbread Fed!" they chanted repeatedly before erupting into a chorus of laughter. It wasn't until the lights from the small town of Karval appeared in the distant horizon that the coaches decided to refocus their attention to the game at hand.

As we rode through the town, we noticed that every store was closed. There was no one out on the streets of Karval. The playful chants and boisterous laughter came to an abrupt end and were replaced by looks of bewilderment and blank stares. We struggled to find a spot in the school's parking lot. It seemed as though the entire population of the town of Karval had shown up to support their team. When we opened the doors of the van we could hear the bass drums from the pep band beating vigorously. Our players looked at one another apprehensively, wondering whether we had mistakenly arrived at the wrong place. Walking into the gym, we noticed that the lights seemed a lot brighter than normal.

The stands were filled to the rafters with adoring Karval High fans, and the atmosphere was electric as the Trojans warmed up on the court. As our players dressed for the game, Coach Rex began his pregame speech, hoping to encourage the team. From the opening tipoff to the final buzzer, the Trojans took us behind the proverbial woodshed as we suffered our worst loss of the season.

In whatever you do, don't allow selfish, arrogant pride to be your guide. Be humble and honor others more than yourselves (Philippians 2:3). Wow, what a lesson learned that day: We must never underestimate an opponent. As Paul reminds us in Romans 12:3, "For I say, through the grace given to me, to everyone who is among you, not to think of himself more highly than he ought to think, but to think soberly, as God has dealt to each one a measure of faith." In the words of Dr. Martin Luther King Jr., "We must accept finite disappointment but never lose infinite hope."

In his book *Leadership Secrets* Dr. Billy Graham emphasizes that a leader's attitude must be one of resolve, allowing him to press on, to push through pain and disappointment. Studies reveal that negative thinking drains a person, while positive thoughts energize and raise the level of one's capacities. We must face the reality that the path to purpose involves discipline and pain. As God directs us through Paul in His holy Word, "In everything give thanks; for this is the will of God in Christ Jesus for you" (1 Thessalonians 5:18). The best path forward is an attitude of gratitude, for this pleases the Lord. When we have a grateful attitude we gain a better perspective about life because our thinking plays an integral part in our leadership effectiveness.

It is vitally important that we as leaders allow the Holy Spirit to help shape our thinking. If we want to have a proper attitude toward the issues we face, we must have a willingness to yield to the Spirit's direction in any given situation. To develop the right kind of attitude we must dedicate ourselves to study, meditation, and the memorization of Scripture. The brutal reality is that our thoughts are broken and we are inclined toward evil and negativity. We are in dire need of the holy God to help us in our brokenness. When we're able to face and deal with the brokenness in our lives, God qualifies us to help others face and deal with their own brokenness.

Satan's goal is to destroy life and to warp our view of reality and of God. The devil intentionally tries to impact children with negative experiences, trauma, illicit sex, and exposure to wicked influences. Our adversary is clever in exposing wicked things to children, knowing that they'll take what they see and hear literally.

Taken in a positive direction, this same propensity leads to what we call "childlike faith"—a beautiful picture. A child's early years develop their beliefs, values, and personality. Unfortunately, some television programs have become a medium for violence, profanity, and fear. Unchecked exposure to such programming can raise havoc in a home and in a child's mind.

Satan has masterminded a plan to intentionally get us to accept sin and compromise our moral and biblical values. Portions of the entertainment industry and media have desensitized our minds to the compromise of our convictions. Leaders must safeguard their home, workplace, and minds from thinking that can derail their character and purpose.

We need, at minimum, to get back to reading. I like this rhyming quote from an unknown source: "Leaders are readers." Immersing ourselves in God's Word keeps us informed about the past and present and helps us prepare for the future. In *Psalm 101: A Crown of Commitment* James Harmeling states,

> Many followers of Christ provide vile entertainment to be set before their eyes each night on the television screen or computer monitor. Immorality, greed, profanity, false doctrine, rebellion, and overall godlessness are portrayed in most movies today without any discernment on the part of the viewer. A constant exposure to this philosophy dulls one's spiritual appetite and numbs one's conscience.

We must become intentional and creative to place before our eyes influences and suggestions that are healthy for our souls, enabling us to be on the same frequency as the kingdom of light, as opposed to that of darkness.

The late Myles Munroe pointed out that "eagles do not hang around with pigeons." Soaring with eagles maximizes the abilities with which God has endowed us. We'll be more inclined to have a negative attitude if we're hanging around and associating with people with a pigeon mentality. The apostle Paul observes that bad company corrupts good character (1 Corinthians 15:33). Our attitude should lead us to take one hundred percent responsibility for wherever we are at any given point in life. We have to continually relearn the art of waiting on God, of allowing Him to elevate us to amazing heights in Himself.

In the beautiful words of Isaiah 40:31, "Those who wait on the LORD Shall renew their strength; They shall mount up with wings like eagles, They shall run and not be weary, They shall walk and not faint." We as leaders must wait upon and relate to God, who will in response elevate us beyond our comprehension. We can soar when we allow God to change and fix our thinking. I could at various points in my life have chosen to continue wallowing in a victim mindset. But thanks to the Word of God my thinking was elevated to desire more out of life.

When we get to the same altitude and on the same frequency as the Holy Spirit, we will excel, rising to new heights in Christ that exceed our wildest dreams. Caution: The way to higher thinking requires effort. One must devote energy and sacrifice to growing as a person, a believer, and a leader. To gain success requires an understanding of one's life purpose, and to understand our purpose is a continuous process of learning and pressing forward until we discover how to use our gifts from God to gain our breakthrough.

The eagle is a magnificent bird, one that loves the storm and can climb up to ten thousand feet in seconds, using that storm as lift. Allow your own trials, the storms of your life, to give you a lift, understanding that enduring trials produces strength of character. Develop the mindset that problems, hard work, and discipline are friends that lead to success. Eagles use the pressure of the storm to glide higher without having to use their own energy. They are able to do this because God created them uniquely, with the ability to lock their wings in a fixed position in the midst of storm winds. This same resolve must be in us as leaders: We must fix our thoughts and attitudes on God's Word; no matter what we see and feel around us, we need to maintain focus and go with what God is revealing to us. When we fix our thoughts on His Word and allow His Spirit to guide us, we will elevate above the storms of life. No matter how fierce your situation may be, trust God to help you rise above the storms.

I challenge you not to run away from trouble, including personal, family, and marital problems. Face it with the help and grace of God. Face life with love, knowing that it's too short to waste on bitterness harbored in your heart. Face your problems with prayer and with the help of family, pastors, and qualified counselors. In your distress turn to God for rest for your soul, and He will help you through the upheaval. Leaders must fight for what's right and avoid checking out, either emotionally or mentally. Let the promises of God's Word propel you upward in Christ Jesus.

Jesus faced the trial of his life; beaten, persecuted, and wrongly accused, He allowed Himself to be crucified on Calvary's cross, knowing that His willingness to face the issues before Him would liberate the human race based on people's acceptance of Himself as Lord and Savior. We have to allow the Father to help us do the right thing so that we may remain standing with Him. Too often Satan deceives us into thinking we need to extricate ourselves from our situation, to isolate ourselves from everyone else. This temptation is one of the devil's oldest ploys, meaning that we must be careful whom we listen to and what we allow to influence our minds and hearts. Yes, there are appropriate times to get away to pray and be in a place of solitude to clear your minds. But escape and avoidance are ineffective techniques when it comes to life's trials. There will be times in the life of every leader when we need to deal directly with our problems in the presence of family, spouse, peers, pastors, or counselors.

I first became intrigued with eagles one rainy July day when I found myself at one of my favorite places, called Praise Mountain, writing and praying. I spent most of the morning in the cabin working on this book and declining to venture outside because of the rain, which was of the soft and quiet, soaking type. The saturating rain served as a metaphor for my thoughts about this manuscript, the message of which had been soaking deep into my soul for several months. When the afternoon came I noticed that the rain was beginning to stop and decided to venture outside for a walk in the light drizzle. I began to trek toward the east and enjoyed a time of praise that lasted a little over an hour.

Deciding to head back to the cabin, I relished the sun coming out and appreciated the heat on the back of my jacket. As I turned south, walking out of the trees, I was startled to observe a huge shadow of wings moving across me. Gazing upward, I caught sight of an eagle about fifty feet above me. I was amazed at the beauty of its spread wings and of the fractured sunrays flowing through them. Hurrying back to the cabin, only about twenty yards away, I retrieved my phone to attempt to snap a picture of this mesmerizing sight. The sun was too bright, however, and I had to find cover. By the time I was prepared to take the picture, the eagle had elevated itself very high and disappeared into the clouds. Wow!

I wondered about the meaning of this experience, about what the Lord wanted me to see and learn. Since then I have researched eagles and, of course, gone on with life and put the experience to the side. But while I was in Fredericksburg, Virginia, on a friend's six-acre property, I found myself outside alone, enjoying the scenery, when once again an eagle appeared above me, circling around before disappearing into the trees. Another Wow! moment. What did this mean? The eagle's ways and life are different from those of all other birds, especially in that eagles fly higher than any others. To elevate our leadership we must develop a certain way of life and thinking that distinguishes us and sets us apart for God's presence. He shifts our thought patterns and lifestyle so that we become healthy, and healthy thinking elevates us to new heights in Christ and creates amazing paths for success.

In the words of Proverbs 1:5, "A wise man will hear and increase learning, And a man of understanding will attain wise counsel." It's a proven fact that your attitude, your pattern of thinking, determines your altitude. We must get the right coordinates, the right frequency, and proper acceleration and thrust in order to take flight. In the Bible we learn about an amazing leader named Joseph, a man of God who had a remarkable ability to solve problems, along with prophetic insight in interpreting dreams. These gifts and the mantle of leadership were given to him by God, and he had an amazing ability to be used of God no matter the environment or circumstances, managing to rise to the top of his game even when the odds were stacked against him. Joseph affords us an example of turning our problems into opportunities to glorify God.

Another amazing leader named Daniel knew how to solve problems by going to the problem solver. Daniel understood that seeking God and developing an intimate relationship with Him would release specific keys to unlock success in the midst of despair and potential destruction. I knew already as a high school student athlete that if I wanted to be successful I needed to change my attitude about education and associations. I grasped that if I wanted to be successful I would need to develop a better work ethic and learn to listen to my teachers and coaches. Associations are vitally important. If you associate with lazy people who have no vision or desire to grow, you will have to make difficult adjustments in order to elevate to the next level. If you hang out with pigeons and chickens, you'll act like a pigeon or a chicken. But if you associate with visionaries and eagles you'll elevate your position. When you use your gifts and abilities with excellence, you will enjoy life and have a shine upon your life that won't go unnoticed.

I am glad that my father, Wester Ervin Tonkins, modeled hard work. He was employed by the same company for forty years—almost unheard of in this day and time. My dad was consistent in getting up at the same time each morning and having coffee and breakfast with my mom. They would converse in sign language before he headed to work. He worked hard on the weekdays and even tackled a second job on the weekends. The only time I remember my dad missing work was when he had been injured on the job—bitten by a bulldog when on a delivery. Unable to hear the dogs barking, he didn't realize they were getting ready to attack him. He endured several stitches and explained to us in graphic detail how the dog had attacked and refused to let go. Despite the severity of his injury he returned to work as soon as he could.

Standing alone as a leader can be difficult. Notice, however, that eagles often soar alone. When training for football I remember being outdoors on cold and rainy evenings with no other persons in sight. I remember thinking that all the other people were inside in the comfort of their cozy houses, watching television and enjoying a good meal, while I was out here in the elements, tired, cold, and hungry. I resonate with the adages "No pain, no gain" and "No sacrifice, no success."

In time the hard work paid off. My private study and training produced public success in the classroom and on the football and track fields. More importantly, I learned social skills and was able to get along with people of all backgrounds and encourage others in doing what's right. These timeless principles will help elevate you, too, to new heights of excitement and adventure if you're only willing to invest in yourself by working hard at developing the gifts and talents God has given you. To excel you must work hard . . . and sometimes alone. Proverbs 22:29 asks, "Do you see a man who excels in his work? He will stand before kings; He will not stand before unknown men."

I believe that the Lord impressed upon my heart that He was getting ready to take Vickie and myself higher in our leadership. During that summer we had done extensive traveling and attended several conferences. At the National Day of Prayer conference in Washington, D.C., Vickie was privileged to be the guest soloist, singing during both the day and evening sessions. We met Anne Graham Lotz, the daughter of Billy Graham; attended the Republican National Convention in Cleveland, Ohio; and saw Donald Trump accept the Republican nomination. It was a tough summer with so much travel, but we made lots of connections, sharing our concerns with many leaders across America. I believe that God was telling me, "I am elevating your leadership to advance my kingdom through your work."

Eagles rise above the storm and use pressure for additional lift. In order to soar higher in Christ and be seated in heavenly places we must align ourselves with God's Word, will, and way. God is a God of intent, and we must learn to be *intentional* (defined as "purposeful, deliberate, calculated, studied, or preplanned") in our leadership. When we align with God, as revealed in His Word, we get the calibration that helps us align with His heart for all people, races, ages, and creeds.

We dictate the level of our leadership based on the amount of time we invest with God, and we determine our level of insight and our divine destiny by the amount of effort we devote to seeking God's heart. As Paul enjoins us in Romans 12:2–3, "Do not be conformed to this world, but be transformed by the renewing of your mind, that you may prove what is that good and acceptable and perfect will of God. For I say, through the grace given to me, to everyone who is among you, not to think of himself more highly than he ought to think, but to think soberly, as God has dealt to each one a measure of faith."

In Exodus 24:18 we see God capturing the heart and mind of Moses while climbing up to higher ground and waiting in God's presence. Moses received a complete overhaul in his thinking and attitude about his life in God. This higher-level thinking helped him cooperate with God in seeing a whole nation delivered from bondage. God has given us in the form of the Ten Commandments (Exodus 20:7–17) basic guidelines to succeed in life:

1. Have no other gods before me.
2. Have no carved images (idols).
3. Don't take the name of the Lord your God in vain (no cursing).
4. Remember the Sabbath day to keep it holy.
5. Honor your father and mother.
6. You shall not murder.
7. You shall not commit adultery.
8. You shall not steal.
9. You shall not bear false witness against your neighbor.
10. You shall not covet your neighbor's house (don't crave other people's stuff).

To elevate your attitude it helps to follow the example of Moses in the Old Testament and Jesus in the New. Doing so is to go to higher ground, away from distractions, to seek the face of God. The bottom line is that if you want to think differently and elevate your leadership, you must go to God in intimate prayer, learn to worship the Lord, and have communion with Him.

The Bible tells us that Moses went into the midst of the cloud and then up into the mountain, spending forty days and nights in God's presence. Change in our thinking doesn't just happen overnight; it requires the power of God's presence to wash away thought structures that are contrary to His Word and ways through consistent prayer and study of the Scriptures. We must develop a regular habit of going up to meet with God and waiting for a download from the Holy Spirit. When we learn to align with God's heart we begin to view and face battles from a different viewpoint.

Successful leaders don't allow the size of a potential fight to deter them. David, for example, took down Goliath because his confidence and practices were based in God's ability and not his own. Joshua and Caleb had a different attitude because they had a relationship of faith in God's abilities. As for each of you reading this book, your victory and breakthrough will come only through keeping your eyes on Jesus, the author and finisher of our faith. Being in God's Word infuses us with divine confidence to do what would otherwise be impossible for us.

Each of us has a choice. In Deuteronomy 30:19 God challenges His people, "I call heaven and earth as witnesses today against you, that I have set before you life and death, blessing and cursing; therefore choose life, that both you and your descendants may live." We too must opt for life in our words and actions in the midst of a society that is focused on death and destruction. We must be intentional in our actions to make each day full of life and every moment a masterpiece of loving life and enjoying it to the fullest in Christ.

Learning to stay in the vein of life in the midst of negativity, leaders must understand that criticism comes with the territory of leadership. All leaders face disapproval; it's our response that sets each of us apart as an effective, elevating leader. Dawson Troutman reflects that "there is a kernel of truth in every criticism; look for it and when you find it rejoice in its value." In the words of Proverbs 15:31, "The ear that hears the rebukes of life Will abide among the wise."

Leadership Tips:

1. Learn to replace complaining with making requests.
2. Don't blame others for problems you have caused.

Unfortunately, most of us have been conditioned to blame

something, or someone, outside ourselves for the parts of our life we don't like. We blame our parents, our bosses, our friends, the media, our coworkers, our children, our spouse, the weather, the economy, or any other scapegoat that comes to mind. We avert our gaze from the real root of the problem, avoiding the mirror that reflects *ourselves*. Proverbs 4:23 cautions us, "Keep your heart with all diligence, For out of it spring the issues of life." A proper, realistic attitude and mindset will help you enjoy life a whole lot more. Let's all take one hundred percent responsibility for where we are in life—economically, physically, spiritually, and in every other area.

Winning versus Losing Attitudes:

According to Sydney Harris, winners listen, while losers just wait for their turn to talk. Winners make commitments and do their best to follow through. Losers quit when things aren't going their way despite their having made a commitment. Winners admit when they're wrong and have made a mistake, while losers make excuses and try to deflect responsibility. Winners have an excellent work ethic; losers are too busy to do even what's necessary. Winners take the initiative and are intentional in their actions, while losers claim that nobody knows the answer and refuse to research the information. Winners understand that forgiveness is empowering; losers claim to be sorry but hold grudges. Winners keep hoping for a miracle or breakthrough; losers, on the other hand, give up and stop trying. Winners are aware of the morale of their team, while losers think only about their own feelings. According to Harris, successful people in all walks of life, including athletics, studies, work, or play, seem to share special ways of thinking about life that set them apart from the rest of the pack. Winners see things differently than losers, and that is why they win.

Another key to elevating effective leaders is avoiding the attitudes and spirit that engulf the culture with hatred. Again, the founder and author of hate in all its forms, including racism, is Satan. Nursing a negative attitude will hinder and limit your elevation with God. Leaders must recognize that to hate a person based on their color or background is to have a problem with God, who created that person in His very image, with intricate, delightful detail and design. Racism comes from the devil, who hates all races, colors, and creeds. "When a person is bitter, angry, caustic, cynical," observes Robert Courson, "the chemicals produced in your glands flow through your body. They affect your stomach. They affect your heart. They affect your whole being. Bitterness doesn't pay, even if you have a justifiable reason."

The best attitude to have is that of gratitude. When we're thankful for even the simplest things, we appreciate life more readily—an attitude that catches God's attention and evokes His appreciation. To be alive and healthy, having a roof over our head, is in itself a tremendous blessing. My good friend Eric Bray, who moved to Greensboro from Mount Airy, North Carolina, was a new student. He came out for sports, and we became friends quickly. However, one fall evening while practicing football Eric injured his leg. No one realized the seriousness of the injury until after I had helped him get to the hospital. For the next few weeks Eric had to use crutches, and throughout his recovery I helped him with his books and getting from one class to another. Decades later Eric reminded me of this story. I had totally forgotten. He was still thankful for my friendly attitude during this difficult time in his life.

My point is that a cultural focus on being friends with only the people who look and act like ourselves will limit our ability to rise to new heights. God spoke to me in 2006 while I was facilitating a Destiny Camp in Clearwater, Florida, with our good friends Pastor Nick and Elle Panico. The Lord revealed to us that The Destiny Project, Inc. was to become a multicultural, multigenerational, multidenominational ministry. This would require intentionality on our parts in making friends who didn't look like us. We would be obliged to allow God to take us regularly through attitude adjustments to help us keep a proper perspective on His heart for all people.

Attitude Zone:

1. Keep the attitude of gratitude.
2. Endeavor to align your attitude with that of Christ.
3. Remember that your attitude determines your altitude.

How we see hard work determines at least in part how effective we'll become as a leader. Proverbs 12:24 points out that "the hand of the diligent will rule, But the lazy man will be put to forced labor." A proper attitude is vitally necessary for becoming an effective, elevating leader. We are constantly bombarded with thoughts and must work diligently to keep our thinking aligned with Scripture. Reading, praying, studying, memorizing Scripture, and allowing the Holy Spirit to work in areas of my life that needed fixing have helped me become the leader I am today—to my wife, my children, and those God has privileged me to influence for His glory.

Dean Smith has this to say about a selfish attitude: "*One* player's selfish attitude can poison a locker room and make it hard, if not impossible, to establish team work." Attitude is huge in leadership effectiveness; therefore, strive to maintain a positive outlook on life. I once read that the thoughts you send out to others will have a far greater impact on you than on them. Unlike a material possession, when you release a thought or give it to someone else, it also stays with you. It may remain buried in your subconscious mind long after you've "forgotten" it. Like chickens, however, that return to the coop at night, such thoughts may flash into your consciousness when you least expect them. When your thoughts are positive, you never have to worry about the damage you may be doing to yourself through negative thinking. Cheerful, productive thoughts buried in your subconscious mind can bring positive results when they recur, and by their presence they encourage the maintenance of a positive attitude in all that you do.

Elevate Facts:

Freedom to be who God has made you to be—and that includes your flaws and personality quirks.
Accept responsibility for your actions and where you are in life; accept and utilize freely the gifts God has given you to glorify Him.
Confident, ready to take hold of the gifts God has bestowed upon you.
Trust in and rely on God with all your heart.

The Seven A's of Attitude:

1. Assess yourself.
2. Acquire a positive mentality by meditating on Scripture.
3. Align your life with God's Word.
4. Accept God's purpose for your life.
5. Actions speak.
6. Awesome results happen when we are with God, who is awesome.
7. Always acknowledge God, and he will direct your path.

Elevate Questions:

1. How does your attitude affect your leadership?
2. On what kinds of things does God's Word direct us to focus our thoughts (see Philippians 4:8)?

3. What lesson did Coach Rex and Darryl's basketball experience?
4. List some parallels between the characteristics of eagles and those of leaders?
5. What is the definition of **intentional**?
6. In Deuteronomy 30:19, what choice does God give every one of us?
7. What will you do to change your attitude that aligns with God's Word?

Leaders' Prayer:

Father, deliver us from unhealthy thought processes; may we instead be directly linked with your will and ways so we can align our attitude with yours and flow with your way of doing things. Cleanse us from thinking and thought structures that aren't aligned with Scripture so we can elevate to new heights in you. In Jesus's name, Amen.

STEP FOUR
DELEGATION

· · · · · · ·

> "You shall select from all the people able men, such
> as fear God, men of truth, hating covetousness."
> (Exodus 18:21)

We read this story in Exodus 18:14–22:

> When Moses' father-in-law saw all that he did for
> the people, he said, "What is this thing that you are
> doing for the people? Why do you alone sit, and all the
> people stand before you from morning until evening?"
> And Moses said to his father-in-law, "Because the people
> come to me to inquire of God. When they have a
> difficulty, they come to me, and I judge between one and
> another; and I make known the statutes of God and His
> laws." So Moses' father-in-law said to him, "The thing
> that you do is not good. Both you and these people who
> are with you will surely wear yourselves out. For this
> thing is too much for you; you are not able to perform
> it by yourself. Listen now to my voice; I will give you
> counsel, and God will be with you: Stand before God
> for the people, so that you may bring the difficulties to
> God. And you shall teach them the statutes and the laws,
> and show them the way in which they must walk and
> the work they must do. Moreover you shall select from
> all the people able men, such as fear God, men of truth,
> hating covetousness; and place such over them to be
> rulers of thousands, rulers of hundreds, rulers of fifties,
> and rulers of tens. And let them judge the people at all
> times. Then it will be that every great matter they shall
> bring to you, but every small matter they themselves

shall judge. So it will be easier for you, for they will bear the burden with you."

"Leadership is unlocking people's potential to become better." Bill Bradley

"Growth and development of people is the highest calling of leadership." Harvey S. Firestone

"Surround yourself with great people; delegate authority, get out of the way." Ronald Reagan

To *delegate* means to entrust a task or responsibility to another person, typically one who is less senior than oneself. To elevate your leadership, it's imperative that you delegate responsibility. When leaders feel a need to personally lead every department, counsel every person, and make all the decisions, they stifle growth in themselves and in others. Leaders must train, equip, and entrust others with responsibility and leadership. Moses' father-in-law gave him some sound and timeless advice: it takes a team of capable and honest people to jointly fulfill God's divine plan. Leaders must select and release responsibility to other trustworthy individuals, thereby helping others grow while multiplying their own efforts and effectiveness.

When a leader masters the art of delegation, more is accomplished. The customer service specialist Larry Weber had this to say on the subject: "I empower people to make decisions the way I would. When they face any situation with a guest, I tell them to imagine what I would do in the same situation and do that."

The mission statement of The Destiny Project was crafted from the acronym TEAM, standing for Teach, Encourage, Assist, and Motivate. As a result of taking this concept to heart we have been successful in selecting capable leaders who are trained and equipped with the tools necessary to get the assignment done with excellence. We as a mission organization have seen hundreds of people make a public decision to accept Jesus Christ as their Lord and Savior. Effective leaders equip those they lead so that the work can carry on unimpeded from generation to generation. Delegation affords people an opportunity to grow and learn from systems that work.

When I worked for my uncle McKinley Sherrill in his construction business, I didn't always understand why he did things in a certain way. My uncle developed an excellent reputation for delivering great service to his customers for more than fifty years. When I first started working for him my regular job was to take a wheelbarrow and pick up all the rocks from the ground to prepare the land for the growth of lush green grass. This job was tedious and tiring because I would invariably encounter what seemed to be tons of rocks. After the job was finished, though, we never failed to notice grass sprouting in just a short time. I was surprised at how healthy these yards became. My uncle's goal was to remove any obstruction that might hinder the growth of grass. Because he did things with excellence and made sure everyone did their job well, his services were often sought throughout his working days. He modeled hard work and delegated tough jobs so that we fledgling workers could learn.

In the early nineties I worked as a distribution supervisor for one of the largest manufacturers of bedroom accessories in the world: JP Stevens and WestPoint Pepperell. When I first started in this major role I admit to having been like a deer in the headlights. I had to learn quickly in a fast-paced environment. I would start the shift, and because I was responsible for several components of the business it would seem as though before I could blink the shift was over. I had to oversee several other employees, all of whose jobs were vital to the success of the plant. I appreciated my department manager because he explained how certain decisions could cost the company and encouraged me to pay attention and avoid mistakes; if a mistake was made, the goal was to correct it quickly.

A prime example involves a huge mistake I made that came close to costing the company thousands of dollars. On a particularly busy workday my department manager instructed me to have one of the pickers pull goods from the assembly line and wand them into the scanner to locate them in the warehouse. These instructions were given to prepare for a large order, with a value ranging into thousands of dollars, placed by one of the buyers (our customers included Walmart, JCPenney, Sears, and many other department stores). The big mistake happened when one step was inadvertently skipped in the process of retrieving specific styles and colors. The goods didn't go through the main scanner that enters the huge multiple distribution warehouses because when the picker came into the manufacturing area he bypassed it. The main system, then, had no record of the goods that were about to be ordered from one of our major buyers.

When I arrived at work for the second shift the next day my department manager approached me with a look of panic on his face, asking, "Where are those goods that were designated for a special order?" and pointing out that the main system had no record of them. Remembering that the employee had backed his lift truck into the manufacturing department, passing the main scanner before removing the designated goods from the assembly line, I calmly went to this employee and asked, "Did you remember exactly where you put the goods I told you to put in the same area?" Thank God he did! I asked him to quickly retrieve the goods and bring them back into the main scanning area, being sure to enter them into the main scanner and put them back in the location from which he had retrieved them. A few minutes later my department manager returned, relief flooding his face, to report that the order had been successfully filled. Lesson learned! My oversight could well have cost the company thousands of dollars, and I could have lost my job—all on the basis of a simple but potentially costly error.

These types of mistakes have subsequently helped ensure my careful attention to detail, including the importance of having those I lead repeat back my instructions to make sure they fully understand the task at hand. Proper and thorough training of those we lead is vital. When the details are explained and mutually understood, the operation (of whatever nature) runs smoothly and productively. At times it can be challenging to entrust people with responsibility and hope they'll do the job as we would. But trusting others to accomplish a task leads to better and more effective innovation, which in turn opens the door to better quality and efficiency, as well as peace of mind for the leader. If a leader doesn't regularly reiterate expectations, inspect, and paint the vision of where he wants the organization to go, he or she will be in for disappointment because human beings by nature can lose focus and motivation. When leaders can keep those they lead on the same page, much more will be accomplished. Leadership, delegation, modeling, and communication go hand-in-hand.

Leaders must recognize that not everyone will have the same work ethic and produce the same output. So they must model what they want to see in their organization. Leaders must learn to coax the best from all employees, whatever their level of commitment or expertise, without stifling creativity and innovation.

Millennials, for example, tend to have a different perspective on life and work than Baby Boomers. Because the two groups grew up in different times, each with its own specific problems, levels of expectation, and values, their approaches can be strikingly different. I have learned, however, that Millennials, when challenged with certain incentives, can produce higher volumes of work in shorter timeframes because of their savvy ability to maximize the use of technology. This doesn't mean that Baby Boomer leaders have to change their style of leadership, but it is imperative for them to make adjustments with wisdom and understanding, especially when it comes to motivating people who didn't grow up in their era. When we remember to lead by example, those millennials will see our passion, actions, and work ethic and will capture the essence of what it means to lead a successful enterprise. They in turn will run with the vision and carry out the mission.

Delegation requires the ability to discern how to most effectively position the people we lead, based on their individual strengths and skill sets. Delegation basically involves pouring our knowledge into another person so that the bigger picture of the vision can be accomplished at a faster and more efficient pace.

I remember my days at Lenoir Rhyne University when Dr. Glass, a professor in the religion department and advisor for Fellowship of Christian athletes, a man who understood the art of delegation, would each year select new officers. The natural process of leaders graduating and starting their careers required Dr. Glass to look ahead for capable leaders.

Jesus instructed us to make disciples by teaching scripture and helping those we lead to flow and operate within their areas of their gifting. Jim Downey, who is 103 years old and a Pearl Harbor survivor, has shared four laws in the area of utilizing one's gifts: "Discover your gift, dedicate your gift, develop your gift, and deploy your gift." This amazing leader understands the power of using the gifts God has bestowed upon every person.

My own experience as a follower of great leadership has helped me discover that delegating builds confidence and demonstrates that we believe in and trust those to whom we have entrusted responsibility. Jesus delegated and gave gifts to the Church to equip his body to advance the kingdom of God. Our Lord came to earth to equip His people to serve and build up His body for effective and powerful ministry. Jesus delegated the gifts of the Spirit so that we in our turn might walk in His power and set free those bound by the lies and oppression of the enemy.

As Paul reminds us in Romans 12:4–9:

> For as we have many members in one body, but all the members do not have the same function, so we, being many, are one body in Christ, and individually members of one another. Having then gifts differing according to the grace that is given to us, let us use them: if prophecy, let us prophesy in proportion in our faith; or

> ministry, let us use it in our ministering; he who teaches,
> in teaching; he who exhorts, in exhortation; he who
> gives, with liberality; he who leads, with diligence; he
> who shows mercy, with cheerfulness. Let love be without
> hypocrisy. Abhor what is evil. Cling to what is good.

There is indeed a multiplicity of Spirit gifts, which include those of prophecy, serving (the ministry of helps), teaching, encouraging, generous giving, leadership, and mercy and compassion. With respect to all of these abilities, we as leaders must fully understand and emphasize serving people from the foundation of love and going the extra mile in doing so.

Truett Cathy, the author of *How Did You Do It?* has trained the employees at Chick-fil-A in the importance of service; when customers enter a Chick-fil-A restaurant they expect to be greeted with a smile. Further, they expect delicious food, delivered quickly and accurately, in a clean environment—all of which together comprise the first mile—the expectation. Second-mile service is about the heart; bypassing the requirement of making sure customers get what they expect, this level of service entails offering them something more, something that makes them say *Wow!* This might be as simple as the operator placing fresh flowers on the table or offering fresh ground pepper, or even something as minor as the toilet paper in the bathroom being folded in a certain way.

This is an excellent concept, helping customers know they are valued and important. As in this example, leaders must observe and give precise instructions to those they lead. And those who follow must understand the importance of following directions, which is a vital to becoming an effective leader. These two principles are fundamental in leadership.

A rendezvous with destiny: two decades after graduating from high school, I was captivated by an opportunity to coach track at my alma mater, Grimsley High School in Greensboro, North Carolina. It was a surreal moment when I provided the team with a list of expectations and responsibilities similar to those that had been given to me twenty years earlier. The expectation before every practice had been to run a mile—four laps around the track—as a warm-up, stretch out together at the high jump pit, and wait for our coach to give team inspiration and instructions.

In our stretching cadence I used the exact count we had twenty years earlier. We counted "thousand one" up to "thousand ten" and then changed to another stretch, after which we did different running drills to build speed. One technique that had stuck with me involved increasing speed. Our coach would often emphasize doing strides while reaching out as far as possible. He taught us that if a person increases his stride length when running in time, he will also increase his speed.

The team I coached had a repertoire of workouts to keep them busy until I arrived at practice—a little later because I worked across town at a middle school. The middle school and high school had different dismissal times, with the high school releasing at 2:30 p.m. and the middle school at 3:00. I had the assistant coach monitor and lead practice, but each runner was responsible for making sure he did all the warm-ups; we wanted runners to be self-motivated and take the initiative for their development.

In the introduction of our season I emphasized how important warm-ups are to a runner's development and building of endurance. Leaders in any field must be observant in order to notice giftedness, productivity, diligence, and even those who are either serious or clown around. One of the sprinters wasn't performing his best in practice, and I also noticed that he clowned around. In our track meets this particular runner would run decently, though not to his potential. The season drew near to the conference meet to be held in High Point, North Carolina, at Andrews High School. This was a very important meet at which runners should have been nearing their peak performance. Runners were required to qualify with a certain position or time in order to proceed to the next level, and if a runner failed to qualify the season would be over for him. This particular sprinter missed qualifying by hundredths of a second.

His first response after this very close result and disappointing missed opportunity was, "Coach, I should've listened and run the mile at the beginning of practice like you told me all season." This runner admitted that he hadn't taken the warm-ups seriously, resulting in a missed opportunity based on a lack of following simple instructions. My absence at the beginning of practice meant I had been unaware that he'd been skipping the warm-ups.

Case in point to all of us who have been delegated responsibility: if you approach your area of responsibility halfheartedly, the deficit will catch up with you literally. As the coach I took responsibility for this missed opportunity, recognizing that I should have explained in more detail the goals and purpose for specific drills that build speed and endurance. I also should have made certain the assistant coaches were more observant and asked more questions. This is why I'm big on *inspecting* what I *expect*. Our youth need someone to believe in them and cheer them on, also in their race of faith. Jesus has commissioned us to go and make disciples (Mark 16:15). In essence, making disciples and delegation go hand-in-hand.

Approaching the mid-nineties while transitioning our family to Colorado, God gave us as a couple a heart for evangelism. Our life in Colorado was launched by the winning of souls; and we have witnessed an amazing number people accepting Christ as Lord and Savior.

We launched the Destiny Project in 1997 and the Destiny Tour teams in 2001. The training and development of young people were in high gear. The Lord clearly spoke to me about leading teams on evangelistic tours across our nation, using the platforms of sports and drama. From 2001–2016 we were able to witness a generation of young people stepping up to the challenge to be trained and discipled for conducting evangelism across the nation. The teams we trained learned basic biblical fundamentals that helped each person establish a solid foundation in their faith in Christ, and we taught them the importance of developing a life of fasting and prayer. We practiced sharing personal testimonies and witnessing to others in sharing how to accept Christ Jesus as personal Lord and Savior. These young people learned life skills that enhanced their abilities to relate to other cultures and races.

We had strict guidelines—tough and rigorous—for leadership with Destiny, and the young leaders quickly learned that decisions have consequences, as well as that each person's role is vital to the team's overall success. When we would arrive at a location to facilitate a camp, we were often referred to as the army because the team members fulfilled their specific assignments with skill and efficiency. The Destiny team flowed like a well-oiled machine. Preparation in prayer, fasting, and the practice of daily Scripture memorization positioned us to see God move in a powerful way. At the end of every camp we would conduct an altar call in which entire families often accepted Christ as their Lord and Savior. As we put together teams to travel to Florida, year after year we developed a community of friends and a following; kids anticipated our coming each year, as evidenced by new friendships and more conversions. God delegated a mandate to us to preach, teach, and disciple people, and we have done our very best to be faithful to what the Father has asked us to do. I have often stated in my travels that "every mile is worthwhile when one soul accepts Christ as their Lord and Savior."

I am humbled and honored to see young leaders discovering their call while serving on the Destiny team. I want at this point to highlight a key leader, Megan, who reached for more. Megan had the opportunity to participate in a multiple-year camp with the Destiny Project; to do back-to-back years with Destiny camps is amazing due to the high level of commitment and the rigorous training that are involved. Megan recognized her passion for missions and answered the call of God to go into the field. She also captured the heart of how Vickie and I collaborated with marriage and ministry. We were deeply honored by Megan's request for me to officiate her wedding. Megan qualifies as an elevating, effective leader who has impacted many for God's glory.

We are truly grateful to the many young leaders we had the privilege to train and are blessed when they come back to thank us. Those who do this understand relationship and receive a deeper substance of leadership. I call this the ten percent principle. The Bible says that Jesus healed ten lepers but that only one returned to say thank you. Jesus asked about the whereabouts of the other nine. Because this person did return, he received a greater blessing and was not only healed physically but made completely whole.

When an individual goes back to say thank you to those who have helped them grow and develop, both parties experience a special bond. The attitude of gratitude gets God's attention, and God blesses the thankful heart. The best gift we can delegate to those we lead is our modeling for them a life of prayer, the devoted study of Scripture, and walking with integrity and genuine love for God and people. In Acts 6:4 we read of giving "ourselves continually to prayer and to the ministry of the word." Most of us are ready and even eager to read and study God's Word, but Paul exhorts us to give ourselves to prayer first—let us ever be mindful to make prayer a priority.

I've been blessed to be a part of great organizations such as those that have sponsored the National Day of Prayer and to have worked at Focus on the Family under the leadership or Dr. James and Shirley Dobson, not to mention having experienced the awesome privilege of working for the Billy Graham Evangelistic Association. Through the lens of my involvement with these amazing organizations, I can clearly see that delegating is vital to evangelizing our nation and world. To accomplish assignments of this magnitude for God requires building teams and conferring specific responsibilities as we coach team members along. To delegate effectively and achieve maximum results, leaders must communicate their goals clearly, effectively, and in a timely manner.

Delegating effectively requires four things:

1. Mutual vision: Leaders must see the big picture.
2. Mutual expectation: Leaders must have expectations of each other.
3. Mutual contribution: Leaders must be willing to make the same levels of sacrifice.
4. Mutual commitment: Joshua and Caleb came into agreement in believing that the people could conquer their enemies.

Leaders must develop disciplines that protect them from the ambushes of the enemy; this is why they must be careful not to wear themselves out, as Moses' father in-law explained at the beginning of this chapter. Fatigue leaves us vulnerable—an easy target for attack. We must ensure that we receive proper rest and exercise in order to maintain good health, both physically and spiritually. The United States army has four core principles used for maintaining healthy soldiers: Soldiers must have (1) a family outlet in which they are affirmed and loved; (2) a social outlet, with friends to talk to who understand them; (3) an exercise outlet, such as jogging, recreational sports, or working out to help them release stress; and (4) a spiritual outlet in which they attend church, participate in Bible study, pray, and receive spiritual guidance and support. All four principles are vital for helping soldiers succeed.

To lead effectively we must first learn the art of leading ourselves. Proverbs 25:28 observes that "whoever has no rule over his own spirit is like a city broken down, without walls." We must discipline ourselves to develop excellence in every area of our life, so that we can be enabled to disciple and delegate what it is we want to impart to those we lead. When leaders control their behavior, attitudes, actions, and habits they become more effective. But when they lack control, nurse bad attitudes, or indulge in destructive habits, the effects will spill over into those they lead, leaving a trail of damaged followers.

Delegating involves trust; if we want to be trusted we must be trustworthy ourselves. In addition, leaders must learn to let go of what they hold dear. Delegating involves allowing others to develop their own leadership abilities. The availability of trustworthy and faithful supporters is key to successful delegating.

We must be wise when entrusting leaders with information. If we don't want specific information shared, we shouldn't share it with anyone in the first place; don't ever say something you don't want repeated to anyone else. Trust that internal alert that you get with people, and don't ignore that impulse check from the Lord.

Make sure your training methods and teaching are simple and easy to remember. Leaders need to remain consistent in their leadership in order to effectively disciple. Always remember, too, that the way you look and carry yourself are a part of your message. Be passionate about God, be real, be yourself, and love your family deeply. Delegating responsibility in essence *is* discipleship; Jesus gave Christ-followers a mandate in Matthew 28:19–20: "Go therefore and make disciples of all the nations, baptizing them in the name of the Father and of the Son and of the Holy Spirit, teaching them to observe all things that I have commanded you; and lo, I am with you always, even to the end of the age." Jesus directed us to make disciples, teach them to obey the Word, and ensure those we train that He is with them.

Elevate Facts:

Freely receive and freely give to help people succeed.
Allow growth by delegating and equipping.
Calling—delegate to people who feel called to your work.
True—stay true to the vision by imparting it to the next generation.

Seven D's of Delegation:

1. Decide to whom to delegate responsibility.
2. Discipline yourself to be organized.
3. Duties must be clearly understood.
4. Deliver your best every day.
5. Deadlines help you meet your goals.
6. Discern God's heart in choosing leaders and workers.
7. Delegate whatever needs to be delegated.

Elevate Questions:

1. What have you learned in this chapter about delegation?
2. What seven gifts did Jesus delegate to the body of Christ?
3. Why are details vitally important when delegating duties?
4. Why did Moses' father in-law warn him about the importance of delegating?

5. Why is it hard to delegate tasks that are important to you?
6. What did Jesus delegate to the church (see Ephesians 4:11–12)?
7. What happened to Coach Rex when he missed one detail as a supervisor at JP Stevens?

Leaders' Prayer:

Father, give us the wisdom and insight to discern and select Spirit-filled and capable workers who will advance your kingdom with integrity, wisdom, skill, and excellence. In Jesus's name, Amen.

STEP FIVE
ENDURANCE

· · · · · · ·

"We also glory in tribulations, knowing that tribulation
produces perseverance; and perseverance,
character; and character, hope." (Romans 5:3–4)

"Be a life-long learner; read as many books as
possible." Nelson Mandela

Endurance may be defined as "steadfastness, constancy, patience, or the fact or power of bearing with an unpleasant or difficult process or situation without giving way." The process of writing this book has required much effort and endurance, primarily because in March 2016 I was rear-ended while sitting in my car at a traffic light. I didn't see the car approaching, and the whiplash and force caused a blow to my head, resulting in a concussion, the magnitude of which I didn't immediately recognize. It didn't take long for me to notice, however, that I was finding it difficult to function in several areas I had always taken for granted. The concussion affected my relationships with family, causing me to become agitated and angry over minor issues. My work output plummeted from high productivity to near zero; I would sit at my computer stymied over how to open a document. My driving was impacted, leaving me exhausted from driving just seventy miles to Denver. My joy and excitement over life were altered to the point that I wasn't laughing at all.

The biggest surprise came when my wife noticed my struggles to maintain my balance. I was in the habit of practicing an exercise in which I would stand on one foot for thirty seconds but found that I could no longer do this simple exercise proficiently—or at all with

55

my eyes closed. For me as an athlete this once simple exercise that had required hardly any effort became difficult and frustrating, to the point that Vickie and I both knew something was seriously wrong.

We discovered that the part of my brain called the cerebellum, which helps control impulses and manages balance, was bruised from the accident. My cerebellum had noticeable swelling, and at times it seemed as though I could feel the fuses around my cranium moving. Another frustration in trying to write this book was my inability to put together my thoughts as I had before the accident, when I was writing fluently, with lots of creativity and no end of exciting examples for this book. After the accident this became an arduous and frustrating journey, though I kept on reading and writing as best I could.

At that point the Lord impressed upon my heart to go on a speaking and book tour. I foresaw that this would be a challenge, since I wasn't as sharp as I would like to have been in my thought processes. The prospect of distance driving seemed daunting, though I knew that flying would also be challenging due to the effects of being in a pressurize plane.

My first experience with flying after my accident had been to North Carolina in April 2016 for training with the Billy Graham Evangelistic Association. In all my prior years of traveling I had never experienced a problem with airport security. While going through security on that occasion, I went through the normal procedure of taking off my shoes and belt, emptying my pockets, removing my sport coat, readying my licenses for inspection, loading everything in buckets, and putting it all onto the belt to be scanned before proceeding through the body scanner. Afterward I hurriedly put on my shoes and belt, returned everything to my pockets, and grabbed my bag—or so I thought. When I departed the security area in the Atlanta airport, however, I sat down with all my stuff, only to hear my name over the airport intercom system. Mystified at being paged to return to the security area, I arrived with my stuff—and with a headache.

A security agent asked me. "Did you leave anything, Mr. Tonkins?" I responded, "Not to my knowledge," after which he asked me the same question. Repeating my response, I inquired why he was asking, upon which they rolled my carryon suitcase over to me, opened it, and asked, "Is this yours?" I had completely spaced out, leaving behind my suitcase packed with my books on prayer. I couldn't believe I had been so completely clueless as to leave my luggage in security. The alarming aspect of the situation is that each time I have flown since that day I have lost something while going through security.

My concussion-assessment specialist told me that the alpha and beta levels on the right side of my brain were off the charts, to the point that it was a wonder I had been functioning at all. I realized that only by the grace of God had I been kept safe. I also needed glasses with corrective lens to help get my vision back to center, the concussion having resulted in "ambient vision." The new glasses gradually centered my vision through a series of prescription lens helps.

Jesus warned us that in the world we will have trouble but invited us to be of good courage because He has overcome the world. I must say that it took a lot of courage to keep moving forward and am happy to report that with God's strength I have fully recovered. The amazing thing about all of this is that I had played college football and never experienced anything like what I endured decades later from this car accident.

To be an effective leader one will definitely need the byproducts of endurance and patience. As Paul told his younger protégé, Timothy, in 2 Timothy 2:3, "You therefore must endure hardship as a good soldier of Christ Jesus." Coming up through the ranks as a student athlete and being appointed to leadership roles again and again, I've become accustomed to hardships, to getting knocked down by life and learning to get back up. I also fully recognize that it is God who gives me the strength to get back up when life literally knocks the breath out of me. We have to rely on God's help to keep us from slipping due to failures, fatigue, and major setbacks, and we must at times be infused with an extra dose of divine strength to stay the course in Christ Jesus. Prayer is a mighty force that keeps us going when the enemy tries to knock us off course. In the words of the psalmist in Psalm 17:5, "Uphold my steps in Your paths, That my footsteps may not slip."

I love to paint the picture of how endurance has helped me develop strength of character through my high school track experience. My sophomore year in high school I found myself among veteran student athletes who were juniors and seniors. I was assigned to the relays, and we set school records in both the 4X100 and the 4X200. My responsibility was to run as fast as I could and make sure I had a clean baton exchange. Running these 100 and 200 sprints as part of a relay team made me look good. But now I had a problem: my coach said he wanted me to begin running the open 400 meters—an event in which no one wanted to participate. I pleaded with him not to have me run that race, but he was insistent. The bigger challenge was that the race was to be run indoors at the University of North Carolina at Chapel Hill. Athletes from around the state would be running in this track invitational—my first individual race of the season.

As I prepared at the starting line I had no idea what to do—other than run as fast as I could. Since this track was indoors it was smaller, with two-and-a-half laps equivalent to one full lap of 400 meters. When the gun fired I sprinted out as fast as I could. I was leading on the first and second laps, but on the last half-lap my body began to get tight, to the point that I could hardly pick up my feet and was out of breath; the most embarrassing aspect was that I almost fell off the track and ended up coming in last place. This painful and embarrassing experience left a desire in my mind to have nothing further to do with this terrible event. I didn't want to ever again have to run this race. However, my coach continued to assign me to the 400 meters. Looking at him in consternation and surprise, I would ask incredulously, "Did you see how bad I did?"

I didn't win in the individual races in the 400 meters for the entire season. However, three years later, in my senior season, I came to understand what my coach had wanted to accomplish in me. To my surprise I became a strong 400-, 200-, and 100-meter runner, the champion in conference, in sectional, and in regional, and the runner-up in the State meet held at North Carolina State University. I had no idea this would happen, but my coach foresaw the outcome because he knew the process of developing endurance and strength. I am still thankful to Coach Russell Woodward for helping mold me into the leader I am today.

In summary, the process of building endurance—physically, mentally, and spiritually—can start out looking like failure. I failed my way forward and ultimately became a success. Thomas Edison attempted the creation of the light bulb, failing countless times before finding the right formula; now, decades later, we enjoy lighting in our homes, cars, and cities. Because of one man's relentless effort and refusal to give up, our lives have literally been lit up. Abraham Lincoln ran for office multiple times, failing to the point of suffering a nervous breakdown. However, he got back up each time and tried again . . . and became one of the most effective American presidents of all times.

Endurance is an essential characteristic for leaders. Hebrews 10:35–36 exhorts us to remain confident and not quit: "Therefore do not cast away your confidence, which has great reward. For you have need of endurance, so that after you have done the will of God, you may receive the promise:" Life's challenges help us keep an eternal perspective to remain faithful until our Lord and Savior returns for us. Endurance helps us resist the urge to quit when we're hit with physical and spiritual battles, enabling us instead to hold on to our faith in Jesus Christ.

Hold on, my friends, training your focus on Christ Jesus, the author and finisher of our faith. When He arrives we will receive our glorious crown. Jesus made it clear that the one who endures to the end shall be saved. Effective leaders lead by example, enduring for the sake of their family—including all those in the body of Christ. Paul's exhortation in Ephesians 6:10, "Finally, my brethren, be strong in the Lord and in the power of His might," is key to endurance. And Acts 17:28 reminds us that "in Him we live and move and have our being, as also some of your own poets have said, 'For we are also His offspring.'"

Many of us have experienced unimaginable hardships. May our Father continue to infuse us with the hope, love, and faith to press onward toward the goal of our high calling in Christ Jesus. I challenge you to continue to go deeper in Christ so that you may one day be elevated to sit in high places with our Lord and Savior. Leadership requires patience, and endurance. When we keep on moving patiently forward, we will began see endurance that has been developed transition into enthusiasm. My pain and embarrassment on that track in Chapel Hill three years prior later turned into enthusiasm because I had worked, enduring pain and hardship to get to the place where running became a pleasure and pushing myself forward into success in college. Paul enjoins us not to be "lagging in diligence" but to be "fervent in spirit, serving the Lord" (Romans 12:11).

Enthusiasm comes from the Greek *entheos*, which means to be filled with God. Being enthusiastic about your work and calling is essential in your leadership effectiveness. When you're enthused about your work, that passion catches fire with those you lead. Enthusiasm gives birth to a natural synergy that will catapult your vision into the future. Working with energy and enthusiasm allows people to glimpse the nature of God.

When a leader has a vision that is from God and communicates that vision with conviction, an atmosphere of enthusiasm is birthed. Vision is one of the key characteristics common among effective leaders. When a leader is excited and works hard, this translates into others becoming excited and working hard. And when people get excited about joining God's great adventure, great things happen. In my college days I was known for saying "You gotta believe!" and I said it with confidence and enthusiasm.

Story of God's Amazing Provision:

I have a lot to be excited about. In demonstration, I would like to take you back to the time I started dating my Vickie. I met her during my favorite time of the year: the fall, during which I loved the cooler temperatures and the opportunity to play college football. I met Vickie for the first time at Optimist Park in Hickory, North Carolina. I started liking her very quickly and knew early in the relationship that I wanted to marry her. But with my being in school and playing football I knew it would be a while. Yet God's ways are higher than ours, and as we began dating leaders around us were making predictions that we would get married soon— as in not waiting till I had finished school and secured a job. We ourselves didn't see this as a possibility, but as we began to seek the Lord we started sensing impressions from the Lord that we would marry earlier than we had thought. I advised Vickie that if my pastor approved we could consider an earlier marriage, after which I would have to talk to my coach—not to mention, of course, Vickie's father.

That journey began one fall day in 1986 where I drove to Greensboro for a scheduled appointment with Pastor Otis Lockett, Sr. on Dillard Street. We sat out on the front porch in two metal folding chairs, and Pastor Lockett asked me, "So, what's going on?" Before I even asked the question I was convinced that he wouldn't recommend our getting married so soon, especially since I wasn't employed and was still in school. I was ready in advance to accept— and follow—his counsel.

Here we go with my question: "Pastor Lockett, I want to marry Vickie and want to know your thoughts about this." He leaned back in his chair and paused for a moment, looked at me, and responded, "That would be good." I was completely surprised, not having expected this affirmation. Wow! He went on to say that he wanted to meet with both Vickie and me. I drove back to Hickory surprised and excited at the same time.

My next meeting would be with the head football coach at Lenoir Rhyne. Asking to speak with him as we neared the gymnasium, I asked a similar question to the one I had posed to Pastor Lockett. Amazingly, he also paused, leaned back, and pronounced the word "Good" before directing me to the office that handled housing for married couples. He shared his prior knowledge that a unit would soon be coming available—another Wow! When I arrived at the office they informed me that our housing would be covered under my football scholarship. Another shock! Before we married I had the blessings of my two primary leaders, along with a place for myself and my new bride.

My third meeting, of course, was to be with Vickie's father, at which I would ask for his permission to marry his daughter. Vickie's father, leaning back in his comfortable loveseat, gave a nod of agreement and also verbalized his approval. We became engaged within a few months and were married within ten months of our initial meeting. It was exciting to be in school, doing well academically, playing college football, and being married to the woman of my dreams. I am so blessed to still have my sweetheart by my side decades later. God is so good, though I know I don't deserve the lovingkindness he has shown me and my family. Can you understand why I'm excited about Jesus?

I was enthusiastic about Vickie when I dated her thirty years ago, and I'm equally enthusiastic about my wife today. I remember a time when I was dating Vickie and she was to drive alone from Hickory, North Carolina, to Greensboro to visit my family. To ensure that she would make it all right, I promised to meet her in Winston-Salem at a gas station at a specific exit. My older brother Alvin was with me in my 1968 Volkswagen bug. Waiting and waiting, I began to wonder whether she might have missed the exit, so I began traveling west on I-40 to see whether I might spot her traveling eastbound. Obviously, in the eighties cell phones weren't yet available.

As I gazed around I saw her car and announced to my brother, "There she is!" There was a place for service vehicles to turn around, a dirt embankment for four-wheel-drive type vehicles, but I didn't care: I was going to catch my future wife. I spun around at a speed not conducive to Volkswagens off the road, and we went a little airborne through the hilly dirt embankment before turning east to catch up with Vickie. I put the accelerator to the floor, urging my Volkswagen to put on its best performance. Funny thing was, Vickie was on time, waiting at the gas station as arranged. She had witnessed my antic and wondered what I was doing, and we all laughed. My brother commented, "I know you love Vickie," based on my wild display. This is what enthusiasm looks like.

When I coached basketball on the middle school and high school levels, the parents quickly noticed how intense and excited I would become about our players and team. Enthusiasm sometimes comes naturally, while at other times one needs to prime the pump. However, it tends to catch fire when a leader is excited. I've been blessed to coach amazing young people and have experienced amazing games and unlikely come-from-behind victories. A big part of my success as a coach has been in the area of building godly character, physical endurance, and enthusiasm in my players, both about the game and about the budding future leaders they were becoming.

There are important keys in coaching, one of which involves perceiving the strengths both of one's own players and of their opponents. Preparation, including an excellent game plan, is another ingredient that helps build enthusiasm, as is learning to be flexible in making necessary adjustments, while eventually getting back to the basics behind your team's strength. When a team is trained and prepared for execution, high levels of enthusiasm are produced, making the job seem easy.

The Bible describes the Spirit as the *ruach*, the Hebrew term for an unpredictable, wild wind. The Spirit brings ecstasy and exuberance at times but ultimately works through the will. Billy Graham says this in *Leadership Secrets*:

> Leaders must keep their love and enthusiasm for the Lord at the forefront of their lives. John Beck says, "Stay true to Jesus!" Keep your heart close daily and do not be another casualty of getting shot down morally, quitting because of deep discouragement, giving into the pressure from the culture and peers with liberal theology, and becoming money driven. We must be steadfast like Joshua and Caleb. Joshua and Caleb learned three important components of war. Worship God for he is worthy of our praises, align your faith in God's ability, and remember all the amazing miracles he performed in the wilderness. Because they knew the character of God they knew that no matter how things looked, they could put their trust in the Lord. Because they had been battle tested, they knew that God would give them the endurance to finish the battle strong.

Hebrews 12:1–2 reads,

> We also, since we are surrounded by so great a cloud of witnesses, let us lay aside every weight, and the sin which so easily ensnares us, and let us run with endurance the race that is set before us, looking unto Jesus, the author and finisher of our faith, who for the joy that was set before Him endured the cross, despising the shame, and has sat down at the right hand of the throne of God.

God directs us to strip off the weight! What is slowing you down from serving Him with fervor and enthusiasm? Is it your health and eating habits, lack of exercise, or a besetting sin or habit? Whatever it is, make the decision today to do something about the impediment so that you'll be free to serve God with all your heart, mind, soul, and strength.

When we keep our eyes on Jesus and see the bigger picture, we'll discover that enthusiasm keeps the life in the organization.

Elevate Leadership Moment:

I would like to highlight an amazing person, my daughter Victoria. She has had many trials since the very beginning of her life. Doctors told us that Victoria would have spina bifida, and they recommended that we abort her due to the medical complications. You know our answer to that suggestion was a big no because we believe in giving life, not taking it.

Throughout Victoria's life, she has been resilient despite life's difficult challenges. I have been amazed by her giftedness and abilities to do amazing things when she sets her mind to do something. Victoria worked for a charter school called Pikes Peak Prep where she worked in the computer lab as a computer facilitator. This is the location where we also hosted our weekly outreach for Team Destiny.

The principal once called me and told me they were looking for a basketball coach for the elementary level. I asked Victoria if she would be interested in coaching and I told her she would do a good job. I called the principal back to let her know my daughter would be interested. Victoria took on this assignment to coach with seriousness and intensity. She asked for my opinion from time to time. Her focus was making sure that the players were disciplines and conditioned. She only had six players, all of them boys, and she worked them hard.

When she had her first game, she was nervous but ready for the challenge. Her team won the first game, then the second, and the next several games until she came up against a power-house team that seemed to have three times the players and appeared to be three times taller. She also had to deal with the mental challenge of coaching against the school that had an entire coaching staff of men. This regular season game was their biggest challenge.

The team handed Victoria her first regular season lost. Nevertheless, the game was close, which surprised many in the stands. My daughter's team wrapped up their regular season with only one loss, and then it was time for playoffs. They knew they would meet the team again in the tournament championship, but they were determined to be prepared.

As expected Victoria's team met the team in the championship game. This game had everyone on the edge of their seats as the teams battled back and forth for the lead. As time ran down, Victoria's team led with just minutes remaining. Their opponents threw everything at them from zone defense and man-to-man, trying to wear out the six-member team.

The other team's coaching staff was baffled that one coach who was young and female was out-coaching the men who were all old enough to be her father. As Victoria coached with intensity and enthusiasm, pushing her team to endure the onslaught, her foundation of building endurance in the beginning of the season paid off in the championship game in which Victoria team of six won in dramatic fashion.

The principal, parents, and students were so ecstatic that they all felt like they just won the NBA championship. The atmosphere was electric and exciting because six players and a young female coach just dismantled a powerhouse basketball team.

I am so godly proud of my daughter and have thoroughly enjoyed seeing her raise her own daughter in the admonition of the Lord. Victoria is the most giving and loving person I ever met at her age. I know God will continue to do amazing things through her. Victoria name means *victorious* and *conqueror*. Because her faith in the Lord, Victoria is more than a conqueror and her daughter Samantha, our granddaughter, has been a joy in our lives.

Holding up in the midst of adversity and pressure produces a confidence within us, that will prepare us for test down the road. We quickly learn that difficult circumstances helps build within us an endurance to remain poised and stand strong to receive God's promises and be in positions to lead effectively.

Elevate Facts:

Faith is the fuel for leadership.
Adjust your attitude and endure painful challenges!
Concentrate on the goal and vision.
Train yourself to be disciplined, and keep your enthusiasm close by!

Seven E's of Endurance:

1. Endurance gives birth to life.
2. Evaluation helps you monitor your progress.

3. Endeavoring to maintain unity keeps your people moving in the right direction.
4. Energy helps you keep moving toward your goals.
5. Enjoying the journey makes life much smoother.
6. Excellence keeps things flowing upward.
7. Enthusiasm makes others want to join your team.

Elevate Questions:

1. Why is endurance so vital in leadership?
2. How did Coach Rex build his players' endurance levels?
3. How would you identify a leader who has endurance?
4. How did God pave the way for Rex and Vickie to get married while he was still in college?
5. Why did Rex drive his Volkswagen through a dirt embankment?
6. Why should you be enthusiastic about your spouse?
7. When are you going to get enthusiastic about serving God?

Leaders' Prayer:

Father, grant us the stamina and endurance to stay with the path and course you have laid out for us. Help us to keep our footing and not to slip but to remain in step with your purpose and destiny for our life. In Jesus's name, Amen. (See Psalm 17:5.)

READINESS

. . . .

> "Do you see a man who excels in his work? He will
> stand before kings; He will stand before unknown
> men." (Proverbs 22:29)

To *excel* means to be diligent, quick, prompt, apt in business, and skillful. The Greek word translated "excel" means to be over and above, to abound, to exceed the ordinary, transcend, or surpass.

John Wooden, one of the greatest coaches of all times, winning ten championships—more than any other coach in NCAA history—once reflected, "When opportunity comes, it is too late to prepare." When you're in a leadership position, you have to prepare for opportunities to advance the cause of Christ. My favorite saying concerning readiness is "proper preparation produces powerful people." To advance, accelerate, and excel is to align with God's agenda, which brings your readiness to an entirely new level.

Wake up; be ready and alert for God's opportunities. If we're sleepy and lethargic, we'll miss key divine moments to advance God's kingdom. The Greek word rendered "sleep" in the New Testament (*hypnos*) may be defined as spiritual torpor, a state of physical or mental inactivity, lethargy, or decreased physical activity—consider in this regard Luke 9:32: "Peter and those with him were heavy with sleep; and when they were fully awake, they saw [Jesus's] glory and the two men who stood with Him." When we are prayerful and spiritually in tune, we remain in step with God's plans and purposes. Leaders must be ready—physically, spiritually, mentally, and emotionally—for amazing windows of opportunity they might otherwise miss.

Authentic, effective leadership necessitates being ready for anything; I believe that leaders must be prepared physically, in terms of the stamina needed to lead in the days ahead; spiritually attuned with a deep prayer and study life; mentally prepared to address topics with knowledge and skill; and self-controlled with their emotions, maintaining a cool, calm, and collected demeanor when addressing all people, but particularly hostile people in hostile situations.

Being ready and alert for opportunities is vital for being an effective, elevating leader. Dietrich Bonhoeffer once stated that "we must be ready to allow ourselves to be interrupted by God." When God calls you to go into action, you need to be ready without equivocation or delay to execute His plan and agenda.

I recall a time when I played for the Western Carolina University Catamounts, located in Cullowhee, North Carolina. The amazing thing about this time and season was the fact that two freshman running backs, myself included, made the traveling squad to play against Boston College. My trip to Newton, Massachusetts, where Boston College is located, marked my first experience of flying in an airplane. The quarterback for Boston College was Doug Flutie, a Heisman Trophy candidate in 1984.

Coaches from Western Carolina chose two veteran and two freshman running backs. I had anticipated that the veteran running backs would get the majority of the playing time. Because I was still learning the complicated West Coast offensive scheme, I figured I wouldn't play. As I watched the game, I stood up on the bleachers because most of my teammates were taller. I was also fascinated by the play of Doug Flutie, who was only five feet eight inches tall, as well as impressed by the Boston College defense, which included an all-American player at the nose guard: Mike Ruth, who was listed as the strongest NCAA player in the nation. Wow!

The unthinkable happened, however, as I watched our offense: All of the sudden as I stood on the bleachers Coach Bob Waters turned around and looked at me, saying, "Rex, get in the game." I was more than surprised to shift from spectator to participant mode. When I arrived at the huddle Jeff Gilbert, our quarterback, looked at me and called for the sweep play, meaning that I was to get ready to run the ball in a college game for the very first time. The play was to go to the right side; his cadence was *down, set, hike*; and I ran parallel to the sideline, putting up my hands to catch the toss. I quickly turned upfield and to my surprise found myself running five, ten, fifteen, twenty, twenty-five, and thirty yards downfield. I was stopped short of a touchdown by another all-American, who was the safety—the last person to get by on defense. I was told that the Boston College All-American had to dive to catch me, tripping me up and stopping me from scoring on my first ever college carry. An exciting moment because I was ready when my opportunity came!

To God be the glory: I was the leading rusher as a freshman against a top-twenty national team. Even though we didn't win, both David and I were excited as freshmen to not only play but to perform well in a big-time game like that. I was the leading rusher and David the leading scorer, with two touchdowns. David recently recalled that I had predicted on the plane before the game that He would score more touchdowns and that I would rush for more yards, and that's exactly what came to pass. I was with the Catamounts for one season and was privileged to play on the team with players who later went on to the National Football League: Tony Jones with the Broncos and Cleveland Browns, Clyde Simmons with the Philadelphia Eagles, Louis Cooper with the Kansas City Chiefs, and Dean Biasucci with the Indianapolis Colts. That class and team were something special.

Now I want to turn your attention to the Grimsley High School basketball team, an amazing team of young men who made their season exceptionally excellent. My son, Christian, shares his experience of the fall 2007–winter 2008 season:

> Looking back on my high school basketball career, there were many ups and downs during those four years. I would like to think there were more ups than downs. As a freshman I was a starter on junior varsity, as a sophomore a starter on varsity, and appointed captain halfway through the season, and a starter and captain for the remainder of my two years. I saw many losses, many wins, and teammates coming and going. But my senior season I really saw the Lord do something among my team and in me as a leader. Many of the experiences from that time shaped who I am and my leadership style.
>
> Going into my senior season, we were optimistic. We had a good core of about six players returning, and we all had plenty of experience. My family and I have always been a family that prays together, and this year was no different. Early in the morning, around 5:30 a.m., we would get up and pray together. I used this time to pray for my coaches and teammates by name—not only basketball-related, but on a personal level, that God would work in their lives and their families' lives.

The season started out great! We entered conference play at 10–3. We had turned a lot of heads in the sports community of Greensboro, North Carolina. Before conference play we lost a very close game in a tournament that we played in every year. Our team was having a little trouble with one of our teammates. He was being a little cocky about things, he had moments of not listening in huddles, and it cost us a game against a top-ranked team in the state. This tournament is played at the Greensboro coliseum, where thousands of people attended. We were in the championship and had our top-ranked opponent on their heels in this amazing tournament. Many of my teammates were looking to me to say something to the cocky teammate. I kept putting it off, but then finally, with my coaches present, I addressed him on the issues that were hurting the team. He did not take it well at first, but he came around and things were looking bright again.

Conference play was great. We won clutch games that we were expected to win and were able to win the really close games as well. We had games where we came back from behind and also games that we dominated for the whole thirty-two minutes. One particular game stands out. It was against our conference town rival, Page High School, whose mascot is the Pirates. It was a hard-fought game down to the end. We won the game in dramatic fashion by three points.

After the win we were undefeated in conference and locked up the conference title. A big article came out the next day about us. It mentioned how two years before we had finished the season three and eighteen, and now we had done a full turnaround and were eighteen and three. Hard work, determination, and working together as a team had gotten us there. We were a complete team; we all knew our roles and thrived in those. We made it to the sweet sixteen playoffs, and while we did not go as far as we wanted to that year, we finished the season and playoffs at twenty-three and five—one of the best seasons in school history for the Greensboro Grimsley Whirlies. This had not been accomplished in over forty years.

This team was a unified bunch, and I took godly pride in the players' efforts to keep an excellent and humble spirit as young student athletes. The team accomplished something that is rarely done in high school basketball in Greensboro: they defeated every other team in their conference twice. They had a unique lineup, and we never knew who would be the leading scorer, rebounder, defender, or assist leader because they were such a bona fide, unified team.

In 1 Corinthians 10:23 we learn that we have freedom in Christ to do as we want; however, Paul cautions that we should refrain from using our liberty to hurt others and ourselves. We must exercise wise judgment because something we ourselves may be able to handle may be a major stumbling block to someone else. We must not lead people astray by flaunting our liberties because we will give an account to God. Leaders must use their influence to promote life that builds the kingdom.

If you decide to use your freedom in Christ to drink alcoholic beverages, for example, I suggest that you not use that liberty to encourage others to drink. Leaders, in my opinion, shouldn't make alcohol available to loved ones and friends; there are too many casualties from its use and abuse in our culture and society. Statistics clearly show that when people are under the influence they do some very harmful things. I once asked a police officer what motivates a person to pull a gun on an officer, the consequences being so costly. He responded that in the majority of cases people are under the influence of alcohol. Our job as leaders is to lead people to righteousness, not to fleshly and harmful desires. As Daniel 12:3 states, "Those who are wise shall shine Like the brightness of the firmament, And those who turn many to righteousness Like the stars forever and ever."

Leaders must not allow themselves to have their senses dulled but must remain alert and not be naive. In the book of Proverbs we learn key principles from the wisest man of all times, Solomon, though the following nugget comes from a different source, King Lemuel: "It is not for kings, O Lemuel, It is not for kings to drink wine, Nor for princes intoxicating drink" (Proverbs 31:4). I want to point out that the word *intoxicated* may be defined as "to affect temporarily with diminished physical and mental control by means of alcoholic liquor, a drug, or another substance, especially to excite or stupefy with liquor." If you are in a leadership role, you don't ever want to stupefy yourself or others into doing stupid and harmful things. If your soul is often longing for a drink of alcohol, this should be a major red flag. Because one drink easily leads to two and so forth, people often state that they have no idea how they became alcoholic.

The former American president George W. Bush shares his story of alcohol addictions and how he embarrassed his wife and family on many occasions when he became drunk. George W. Bush was in Colorado Springs at the luxury Broadmoor Hotel when he decided to stop drinking alcohol once and for all, realizing that his substance abuse was causing him to abuse his wife and daughters and his influence as a leader.

Lemuel goes on in Proverbs 31:5 to say of leaders, "lest they drink and forget the law, And pervert the justice of all the afflicted." If you're intoxicated, you'll momentarily forget not only the Word of God but who you are in Him. Again in Lemuel's words, "Give strong drink to him who is perishing, And wine to those who are bitter of heart" (Proverbs 31:6).

Are you dying? Are you in anguish? My point here isn't to be critical of those who do drink alcohol but that we as leaders must conduct ourselves in a way that glorifies God. In our culture alcohol is a stumbling block to many, and our young people too often use as an excuse to drink the fact that their parents or leaders drink, making the practice appear acceptable. The reality is, however, that young people don't have the same tolerance and maturity as adults and are less likely to drink in moderation. Young people are wired to do things in excess and too often lack the good judgment to know when to stop drinking.

My biggest concern isn't alcohol per se but the abuse of alcohol that has affected millions and destroyed many lives. If you occasionally savor a glass of wine, do so in the privacy of your home. Paul points out in 1 Corinthians 6:12 that though we're free to do as we desire, liberty isn't always beneficial. Since the days of my youth, and especially during my college years, I have witnessed the effects of alcohol abuse, and in my years as a ministry leader I have helped lead many susceptible individuals to see its harmful results. I hope you who are reading this book can hear my heart and not detect a judgmental attitude.

In my thirty plus years of serving families and ministering to youth, my heart has over and over again been broken upon hearing of the devastating effects of drinking on someone I have known and loved, impelling them to make decisions that have brought destruction on themselves and others. I'm not implying that I'm perfect; I certainly have issues and need to improve areas of my life. But I do want to caution you as a fellow leader to be mindful of how your choices influence others, to pay attention and be sensitive to the leading of the Holy Spirit.

We must use the influence God has allowed us to advance His kingdom, be diligent to be about our Father's business, and help bring solutions to problems. The Word exhorts us (Ephesians 5:18) to be filled with the Holy Spirit (and hence under *His* influence), not drunk with wine. Too many people have been duped into thinking that in order to have a good time one needs to have alcohol. In reality, it's quite possible to have clean, wholesome fun without alcohol. The entertainment industry and beer companies sensationalize alcohol and equate its use with fun and physical attractiveness. But these same companies rarely, if ever, share the harmful effects alcohol brings to the body, the national statistics on causalities on our nation's highways, or how women are exploited—used and abused—while they're intoxicated.

Yes, I'm well aware that this isn't a popular stance among some Christians. In my early years as a Christ-follower I never expected that alcohol would be an issue among believers, nor was I aware of how many believers encourage its use and even provide alcohol at social gatherings. Has anyone ever asked you the question "How do you know when you've had too much to drink?" or "How do you plan on getting home after having a few beers or wine?" Alcohol slows down your senses and alters your consciousness. A person becomes dangerously uninhibited and relaxed and makes rash and unfiltered statements, speaking indiscriminately whatever happens to be in their heart. Satan looks for such scenarios as prime opportunities to devour people.

Leaders can't afford to allow themselves to become intoxicated; doing so will inevitably, and perhaps irrevocably, undermine their testimony in Christ. Those of us in leadership roles must always be alert and ready to follow divine commands and instructions; why give the enemy any ground that could hinder or hamper your testimony?

To be ready as a leader one must realize how the enemy tries to ambush a leader. There are three particular areas in which Satan targets leaders, trying to take them out. "The first ambush and most common ambush," notes Steve Farrar in *Finishing Strong*, "is the ambush of another woman." A well-known Christian coach once shared how he decided to drink a little and before he recognized what was going on found himself in bed with a woman who wasn't his wife. He reported having been so disoriented that he didn't even know who she was. He was full of remorse for his unfaithfulness to his wife.

The second ambush is the lure of money (don't allow chasing money to derail you from pursuing God), and the third is neglect of family. God didn't give us a family in order for us to ignore or neglect them. Leaders must understand the importance of family, must make family a priority by serving them, and must be intentional about being with their spouse and children. Whether or not we realize this, if we aren't serving our families we're missing a huge and important aspect of effective leadership and ministry. "My first responsibility is to my wife," writes Steve Farrar, "secondly to my children. So let me ask you a question, if you are tied up with some woman who is not your wife, what kind of ministry are you going to have to your wife and children?"

One of the key factors for leaders to finish strong is to have a strong accountability team. We must be ready for anything the enemy tries to throw at us, and the best ways to be ready include prayer, staying in love with Jesus, and putting in place accountability partners with whom we can share in confidence concerning our weaknesses and temptations. Two of our friends and their spouses have come alongside Vickie and me to help us see flaws and issues in our life and marriage that we need to surrender to the Lord. God is more concerned about our character, spiritual health, and growth than He is about the work we do for Him. Our good friend Lisa Crump, the chief operating officer for National Day of Prayer, states, "All persons should intentionally position themselves to be accountable to wise others. There is wisdom in a multitude of counsellors." She also notes, "Over time, leaders learn more humility as they realize with each new responsibility, that all ability is truly given by God. Humility is a key factor of a godly leader."

Don't let the enemy deceive you, and don't lie to yourself, assuming that no one will find out about your willful sins and attitudes. There is a law in the Bible stating that your sin will expose itself (and you): "If you do not [arm yourselves before the LORD for the war], then take note, you have sinned against the LORD; and be sure your sin will find you out" (Numbers 32:23). According to Steve Farrar, sin works like this: It (1) can take you farther than you wanted to go; (2) keeps you longer than you wanted to stay; and (3) costs you more than you wanted to pay.

Second Samuel 1:1–2 pictures David excusing himself from the regular annual war campaign and staying home at the palace being idle—costing him more than he could ever have imagined. Yes, God forgave David, but the consequences of his decisions were nearly unbearable for the king; though he repented and received forgiveness, his rash actions still led to insurmountable pain for David and his family. The higher the level of responsibility, the greater the pain for sinful decisions. God forbid that we set in motion destruction and pain for those who love us the most. Protect yourself and your family from the devastating effects of sin. We obviously don't need to live in fear; however, we must rely on God's mercy and grace because we do sin daily, regularly falling short of the glory of God. When we disobey a direct order from our Commander-in-chief we will get ourselves into big trouble. In Deuteronomy 17:14–17 David was given a clear directive from the Lord:

> "When you come to the land which the LORD your God is giving you, and possess it and dwell in it, and say, 'I will set a king over me like all the nations that are around me,' you shall surely set a king over you whom the LORD your God chooses; one from among your brethren you shall set as king over you; you may not set a foreigner over you, who is not your brother. But he shall not multiply horses for himself, nor cause the people to return to Egypt to multiply horses, for the LORD has said to you, 'You shall not return that way again.' Neither shall he multiply wives for himself, lest his heart turn away; nor shall he greatly multiply silver and gold for himself."

The story goes on (verses 18–20):

> "Also it shall be, when he sits on the throne of his kingdom, that he shall write for himself a copy of this law in a book, from the one before the priest, the Levites. And it shall be with him, and he shall read it all the days of his life, that he may learn to fear the LORD his God and be careful to observe all the words of this law and these statutes, that his heart may not be lifted above his brethren, that he may not turn aside from the commandment to the right or to the left, and that he may prolong his days in his kingdom, he and his children in the midst of Israel."

Most people want to be successful! But what is success? Depending on who it is you speak with, you'll no doubt encounter polar opposite views of the word's definition, some based on the world's standards and others on God's. Again according to Steve Farrar in *Finishing Strong*,

> The world defines success in a different way than God's Word defines success. They are diametrically opposed. Worldly success is attaining cultural goals that are sure to elevate one's perceived importance in the culture. Note that word perceived. It does not actually elevate your importance but elevates your perceived

importance. When people are successful by the world's standards, they experience elevation in at least one of three areas: power, privilege, or wealth. Power: Having commands obeyed and wishes granted. Privilege: Enjoying special rights and favors. Wealth: Accumulating financial reserves and securities. The world system talks about success. It is talking about an elevation of status. We must filter through the grid of the Scriptures.

Your character and integrity must keep pace with your accomplishments. We cannot expect something out of our children that does not exist in our own heart. Character is not something you mandate, it is something you model. In addition, if you are chasing after external accomplishments rather than internal character, it will show.

The legendary coach John Wooden, winner of ten NCAA championships, said,

> When opportunity comes, it is too late to prepare. I have discovered that it is best for me to rise early in the morning [and] have my prayer and devotions to prepare myself for God opportunities. Make sure clothes are ironed and ready for the entire week. We have our plans for the day and week but God oftentimes will put us on an entirely different agenda and we must be ready. When we decide to align with God's agenda; this sets you up for success for the rest of the day.

I had the opportunity to meet the Olympic wrestler Brandon Slay, whose signature saying is "Do your best and God will take care of the rest." This Olympic champion learned that it's vital for us to do all we can to prepare and then allow God to take our best to levels far beyond the limits of our imagination.

Being ready means anticipating problems. For example, always do your best to arrive ahead of time for a scheduled appointment. An early arrival allows time for unexpected delays and helps you settle your thoughts to ensure mental preparedness. Being ready means that you have done your homework and studied. As Paul enjoins his protégé Timothy in 2 Timothy 2:15, "Be diligent to present yourself approved to God, a worker who does not need to be ashamed, rightly dividing the word of truth."

Being ready also means having our gear in order—and that includes our spiritual gear: "Put on the whole armor of God, that you may be able to stand against the wiles of the devil" (Ephesians 6:11). Being ready also means being at our workplace at or before the expected time. "Timeliness is important to make sure an organization does not get sloppy," observes George Bush. We as leaders in particular must make an extra effort to be prompt. This demonstrates respect for those who are anticipating our arrival. Being prompt and on time sends a message of respect and avoids being wasteful.

Leaders must prepare for all possible exigencies that might impact themselves, their families, or their organizations. In *Leadership Secrets* Billy Graham notes, "Those who observe leaders conclude that talent and character are measured separately. Talent can take a leader far, but the accomplishments that talent brings also produce great temptations. And talent is not sufficient to sustain a leader's effectiveness if the ever-present human flaws are not addressed."

Leaders must face the obstacles that hinder their leadership effectiveness, and oftentimes we need others to help us deal with issues that can derail us in the future. "Reputations are fragile," notes Bill Pollard. "They must be handled with care like a valuable vase that if dropped can never quite be put together again."

I can tell you from my own experiences as a leader that you'll want to be prepared by being in good physical shape; spiritually alert through prayer and Bible reading; mentally focused, knowing you can do all things through Christ, who strengthens you; and emotionally healthy—for which you'll need the love and support of your family.

An incident standing out in my memory involves an all-star game opportunity that came my way near the end of my high school football career. With just one month to go before heading off to college, I received a call from my coach, Dick Knox, informing me that I had been invited to play in the East-West all-star football game (a game that is played every summer in my hometown of Greensboro). I was obviously elated by the honor and privilege of playing in a game featuring the best athletes from across the State of North Carolina.

When I arrived and began practicing, I was taken aback by my impressions of these elite athletes. In my mind I had placed these players on a pedestal; week after week during football season I had viewed the recorded highlights of their spectacular performances, and I now found myself unable to wrap my mind around the possibility that I might possess a comparable level of skill and ability.

Amazingly, my performance in practice allowed me to rise *above* my counterparts on the depth chart. I went from being an alternate to finding myself in the starting line-up. After each practice the coaches had all the fastest runners on the western squad line up and race. God had gifted me with speed and given me the mindset and determination to cultivate this gift. As a result, on each of the six days we lined up to race I was able to excel, showing myself to be the uncontested fastest player on the team.

The problem was that even though I was excelling physically and athletically on the field, I was failing mentally and emotionally. When game day arrived my mind was still stuck on my perception of myself as a lowly alternate among all-Americans. Looking back, I wish I'd had somebody to tell me it was okay to be an alternate and that I should just go and give my best. I had neither family support nor a familiar coach to encourage or challenge me at this pivotal moment in my athletic career.

As you may have surmised, I didn't manage to step up for the moment during that summer of 1984. This painful and embarrassing experience has taught me the importance of readiness whenever we're offered an opportunity to shine with our God-given gifts. We must JUST DO IT—as Paul charges Timothy, "Preach the word! Be ready in season and out of season. Convince, rebuke, exhort, with all longsuffering and teaching" (2 Timothy 4:2).

By not stepping into the appointed position I missed a great opportunity to shine for my school. I realize in hindsight that this wasn't really about me but was making a statement on a much larger scale. My word to you as leaders: when you're given an opportunity, don't defer because of a lack of self-confidence or courage. If you don't put yourself out there you'll have regrets later on. Grab hold of the moment and allow your gifts and abilities to shine. Don't live in regret but learn from your mistakes and be ready at any moment to lead by example. When you step into your destiny, you encourage others to step into theirs.

In conjunction with my usual policy, I've discovered that it's best to arrive early when I'm leading or speaking at a venue. Doing so helps me settle my thoughts and allows me to get a feel for the environment though prayerful listening for divine guidance.

Peter speaks in 1 Peter 3:15 about another vital aspect of preparedness: "Sanctify the Lord God in your hearts, and always be ready to give a defense to everyone who asks you a reason for the hope that is in you, with meekness and fear." Being ready means preparing yourself for every possible question, objection, or argument that may arise.

"Apologetics" comes from the Greek word *apologia*, meaning

"to give a defense." Leaders must be equipped with wisdom and knowledge to communicate their convictions in a respectful manner. Knowing the truth is important, but even more vital is communicating it in such a way that your listeners will begin to examine their own points of view without feeling condemned or intimidated. In Jude 1:3 the writer says, "Beloved, while I was very diligent to write to you concerning our common salvation, I found it necessary to write to you exhorting you to contend earnestly for the faith which was once for all delivered to the saints." In order to effectively *contend*, godly leaders need knowledge, clear thinking and articulation, tact, and respect.

When you enter a leadership role, you'll need coaches and advisors for your journey. Every would-be leader must count the cost; when you stand up for what's right, be assured that you'll encounter opposition in many forms. To be successful as a leader you'll need to avail yourself of the counsel of seasoned, wise leaders. In the words of Proverbs 24:6, "By wise counsel you will wage your own war, And in a multitude of counselors there is safety." Counsel and preparation are vital allies for a leader. Your strongest ally, of course, is the Lord, so be sure to align yourself with Him through prayer and the study of His holy Word. When we follow the path of God, He will do immeasurably more than we could ever have asked or imagined (Ephesians 3:20–21).

Another important consideration for you as a Christian leader: assess what time it is for you, right here and right now. "And do this, knowing the time, that now it is high time to awake out of sleep; for now our salvation is nearer than we first believed" (Romans 13:11). We're living in critical times, and we must be prepared and ready to answer God's call at a moment's notice. He is summoning us to a higher calling in Himself, and we must prepare ourselves to ascend the hill of the Lord. As David asks rhetorically in Psalm 15:1, "LORD, who may abide in Your tabernacle? Who may dwell in Your holy hill?" His answer (verses 2–5):

1. He who walks uprightly,
2. who works righteousness,
3. who speaks the truth in his heart,
4. who does not backbite with his tongue
5. nor does evil to his neighbor,
6. who honors those who fear the Lord,

7. who swears to his own hurt and does not change (keeps an oath even if it hurts and doesn't change his mind),
8. who lends money to the poor without interest, and
9. who does not take a bribe against the innocent.

"Whoever does these things shall never be moved (shaken)."

Each of us as a godly leader is able to fulfill these principles with the help of the Holy Spirit. Therefore, get yourself ready to elevate, and soar into new places in God.

How can you optimize your readiness? Put on the armor of God daily so that you'll be strong and ready for battle in any given situation (Ephesians 6:12–18). Bear in mind the importance of reputation; as Proverbs 22:1 reminds us, "A good name is to be chosen rather than great riches, Loving favor rather than silver and gold."

Elevate Leadership Moment:

In 2013 our family lived on the west side of Colorado Springs, and we experienced the "Waldo Canyon fire" that caused the evacuation of several thousands of residences. Already when the conflagration was in its early stages, the fire and forestry officials warned certain residents, including ourselves, to pre-evacuate. We were instructed to pack the necessary items and prepare to depart at a moment's notice in case conditions were to quickly change. I am so thankful that we listened to these precautions and loaded our trailer beforehand with vital necessities. When the main evacuation came we were prepared, unlike those neighbors we saw crying in panic because of their failure to heed the precautionary warnings. The fire jumped several ridges due to a storm and blew down into the Mountain Shadows community. This happened so rapidly that it caught the fire personnel off guard. There was thick smoke everywhere, and the only two exits out of the community were clogged with lines of waiting vehicles. The Colorado Springs police department did a fabulous job directing traffic out of those areas in record time.

Once we had arrived at the home of our friends on the northeast side of town, we watched the media coverage. The media, as we know so well, loves to sensationalize events to get the best viewership, and when I watched the CBS coverage of the fire I had to ask myself "Is that *here?*"—the broadcast was making it appear as though the entire city of Colorado Springs was engulfed in flames. The problem was indeed serious, but only the west side of the city was in danger. I was glad we had prepared and managed to evacuate our family without drama from a dangerous situation.

When leaders prepare themselves for life, they exceed their goals: "A wise man will hear and increase learning, And a man of understanding will attain wise counsel" (Proverbs 1:5). And "Because of the transgression of a land, many are its princes; But by a man of understanding and knowledge Right will be prolonged" (Proverbs 28:2). We are faced with many challenges in our world today—far more than I could ever have imagined even thirty years ago. This is why we need leaders with wisdom and knowledge from God for handling and dealing with issues of all kinds. We must drop to our knees and seek a holy God who knows all things and has the solution for all problems.

Elevate Facts:

First to arrive and get to your destination early.
Anticipate and expect attacks and delays.
Creative ways to hone your skills.
Team—promote team readiness and preparation.

Seven R's of Leadership:

1. Ready for opportunities by being prepared early for your day.
2. Real—be the real you God designed you to be.
3. Revere the Lord, for this is the foundation of leadership.
4. Responsibility—taking ownership for where you are in life.
5. Role—follow through with your role as a leader.
6. Reach for the best never settle for less.
7. Regard others with high esteem.

Elevate Questions:

1. What three ambushes are prevalent in leadership circles?
2. Why put on the armor of God daily?
3. What is significant in Jesus's parable about the five virgins who had oil in their lamps (Matthew 25:1–13)?
4. What was the key for David's winning many victories in war?
5. What are some practical ways in which a leader can be ready?

6. What made Daniel ten times better than his peers?
7. How can we cultivate our abilities so we can be ready for God opportunities?

Leaders' Prayer:

Father, please give us divine discernment and divine preparation so that we are always ready for your divine assignments. Lord help us be prepared and alert for we know we have an enemy who desires to kill us, steal from us and destroy us. Thank you for your Holy Spirit that guides us into all truth and helps us in all situations. We thank you for the angels that have been assigned to our life to protect us from harm in Jesus's name, Amen.

STEP SEVEN
SERVANTHOOD

· · · · · · ·

> "He who is greatest among you shall be your servant." (Matthew 23:11)

> "In the military, I learned that 'leadership' means raising your hand and volunteering for the tough, important assignments." Tulsi Gabbard

> "You will never reach your dreams without honoring others along the way." John Paul Warren

The word *servant*, when used as a translation of the Greek *doulos*, means to give up for another, serving as a bondman or slave. To be effective servant leaders, we must daily ask the Lord about His agenda for us and make that their priority. When we align our days and times with God's agenda, we'll be enabled to serve much more effectively.

Leaders too often forget that their first call is to serve their own family. Our actions demonstrate love; we're wise to keep in mind that God is for the family and that He desires for us to be servants who govern our lives and families according to His Word. For the husband, marriage is a continual dying to self, a laying down of his life for the one God has given him. In our society there is an assault on biblical marriage; indicative of the problem is that too few people have an understanding of real love. Love is both a commitment and an action—an acting out of that commitment. Satan has used the entertainment industry to convince us that love is instead an emotion or a feeling. A biblical definition (beyond the obvious, our love of God): love is serving and laying down our life for our spouse, family, and neighbor.

Our children and youth constitute our future, and we must serve and stand up for what is best for them. Too many school curriculums have been designed to convey information that is the polar opposite of that which is right and God-ordained for the family. Serving our God is demonstrated in the actions of prayer, educating with truth, equipping with skills to utilize knowledge, standing up for righteousness, speaking up for truth and justice, and showing up in places where laws influence families and the nation.

Research reveals that no other member of the bird family nurtures its young in the same way the eagle does. Eagles are so attentive to their chicks that they construct hedges around them. We read about a similar, divine tactic in Satan's rhetorical question to God in Job 1:10: "'Have you not made a hedge around [Job], around his household, and around all that he has on every side? You have blessed the work of his hands, and his possessions have increased in the land."

The psalmist proclaims in the name of the Lord in Psalm 91:14, "Because he has set his love upon Me, therefore I will deliver him; I will set him on high, because he has known My name." We as believing leaders owe it to God and to our children (and to those others who depend on us) to protect and rescue them from the deceptions that are so pervasive in our society. Similarly, Proverbs 24:11 enjoins the reader to "deliver those who are drawn toward death, And hold back those stumbling to the slaughter." Leaders must stand up for the innocent, the poor, and the young.

To serve effectively, we must exercise the abilities God has bestowed on us, using these gifts to advance His kingdom. Every one of us must fill the gap by taking up the mantle of service in our divine assignment and role. We have to recognize and activate the gifts that flow into our life. Romans 12:6–10 identifies specific gifts, as follows:

1. The prophetic gift is a special insight from the Lord that reveals information about people and future events.
2. Individuals involved in the ministry of helps facilitate events and projects with a divine flow.
3. The teacher has a special way of explaining truths with details and simplicity, so that learners can clearly understand.
4. An exhorter is a person who naturally encourages people and makes them feel better.

5. The giving person is generous, continuously finding special ways to help and bless others.
6. Leadership is the ability to influence and lead people toward God and His Word.
7. The person with the gift of mercy shows compassion no matter how many times someone has messed up.

These gifts will operate and flow freely when driven by love and faith—when we love and care for people, hate sin, and hold on tightly to that which is good. Serving through love is showing genuine affection; people need encouragement, a handshake, a pat on the back, and affirming words. We are to honor each other, not destroy each other: "Do not be overcome by evil, but overcome evil with good" (Romans 12:21).

A key requirement for being an effective servant of the Lord is faithfulness. In 1 Corinthians 4:1–2 Paul defines his own role and that of his fellow Church leaders as follows: "Let a man so consider us, as servants of Christ and stewards of the mysteries of God. Moreover it is required in stewards that one be found faithful." Servant leaders must exhibit practical skills, such as being on time and prompt; punctuality is a significant mark of leadership because it respects the time of all concerned, and punctuality shows high regard, honor, and respect for others.

As another mark of good leadership, true servants are to be faithful to their wives:

> A bishop then must be blameless, the husband of one wife, temperate, sober-minded, of good behavior, hospitable, able to teach; not given to wine, not violent, not greedy for money, but gentle, not quarrelsome, not covetous; one who rules his own house well, having his children in submission with all reverence (1 Timothy 3:2–4).

Billy Graham notes that we should ask ourselves three questions before we speak: Is it true? Is it kind? and Does it glorify God? And Jeffrey Gitomer suggests that to be the best we can be for others we need to begin by being the best we can be for ourselves. Gitomer highlights three daily requirements to make this happen: attitude, discipline, and self-education.

True and effective servants submit themselves to a holy and awesome God. They recognize deity. In Joshua 5:14–15 Joshua encounters an angelic figure and asks whether he is for Israel or for Israel's enemies.

> He said, ". . . [A]s Commander of the army of the LORD I have now come." And Joshua fell on his face to the earth and worshiped, and said to Him, "What does my Lord say to His servant?" Then the Commander of the LORD's army said to Joshua, "Take your sandal off your foot, for the place where you stand is holy." And Joshua did so.

A vital key to elevating your leadership is learning to humble yourself to follow divine orders.

In 2014 Vickie campaigned to be on the city council; her obedience to God's calling to serve was definitely no cakewalk. In Deuteronomy 30:19 God says through Moses, "I call heaven and earth as witnesses today against you, that I have set before you life and death, blessing and cursing; therefore choose life, that both you and your descendants may live." Vickie and I have chosen to fight for the life of the unborn, the family, marriage between a man and woman, and the biblical foundations upon which this country was established. Vickie faithfully obeyed God in her run for city council and came in sixth place out of thirteen candidates', Vickie compiled over eighteen thousand votes. We didn't win the seat, but we were winners in learning a lot about the great people of Colorado Springs.

Vickie and I both had the adventure of a lifetime; I supported her on the campaign trail and was blessed and honored to serve my beautiful wife. Vickie loved paying attention to the concerns of people in our city, state, and nation. In the words of Robert Courson, "Listening has nothing to do with hearing—it has everything to do with paying attention." The keys we have learned in our years of leading are that we must listen attentively and yield ourselves to the voice of the Holy Spirit so that we can cooperate with God's agenda to advance truth and righteousness.

My favorite college basketball team is the University of North Carolina Tar Heels. The legendary Dean Smith was an amazing coach who knew the importance of players working together and serving one another. Smith stated that "basketball is a beautiful game when five players on the court play with one heartbeat. To serve effectively, everyone must be on the same wavelength and frequency, each knowing their roles and the objective at hand."

Coach Smith once told Michael Jordan, "Michael, if you can't pass you can't play." In the words of Jesus, "If anyone desires to be first, he shall be last of all and servant of all" (Mark 9:35). We could paraphrase this as follows: if we can't serve we can't lead. Dean Smith urges us as leaders to "praise behavior you want repeated." We must recognize those who are faithful servants and promote servant leaders.

In his book *The Rumsfield Way: The Leadership Wisdom of a Battle-Hardened Maverick*, Jeffey A. Krames quotes Donald Rumsfield as saying, "The strength that matters most is not the strength of arms but the strength of character, character expressed in service to something larger than ourselves." Rumsfield also says, "Never underestimate the importance of listening: Remember that the art of listening is indispensable. Effective leaders listen before they act." He further states that every leader should:

1. Be yourself.
2. Speak your mind even if it means making people uncomfortable.
3. Don't be afraid to say "I don't know."
4. Use humor even in tough times.
5. Under promise and over deliver.
6. Don't declare victory until the objective is met.

We can serve more effectively as leaders when we clearly communicate. *Communication* may be defined as "the imparting or exchange of information; the act or process of using words, sounds, signs, or behaviors to express or exchange information, ideas, thoughts, and feelings." The Greek word for communications is *koinoneo*, which means to share, communicate, contribute, and impart. You may be surprised to learn that sixty to ninety percent of all communication consists not of words but of body language, eye contact, facial expressions, and tone.

Leadership requires that we humble ourselves before others and apologize when we have offended them. In 2004 we moved back to North Carolina so our son could attend my alma mater, Grimsley High School. Christian's height was around six feet three inches, and he was noticed instantly by the basketball coaches when he arrived on campus. In the 2007–2008 school year the football coaches asked me why my son wasn't playing football, since I had become something of a football legend at Grimsley. I simply told them that I wasn't going to force my son to play football, since his passion was basketball. If he wanted to play, it would be his decision. They asked whether they could talk to him about trying out for quarterback, to which I agreed.

My son was excited about the opportunity and went to the practice; I was at home relaxing with my wife and daughter. When Christian arrived home he reported that "they tried me out at tight end." Mystified, I informed my son that the coaches had never mentioned tight end—a position requiring as much physical contact as that of a linemen. I called the coach about my concern. After responding that it was none of my business he hung up the phone, refusing afterward to pick it up.

I knew that I would have to pay a visit to his classroom for an explanation . . . and wondered whether he treated other parents in this manner. Not only were we employed together at the school, but I had been reaching out to him in my role as parent. The next day, as planned, I walked to his classroom before classes began and asked him what was going on. He responded by repeating the same question back to me, seeming very surprised at my having a problem with his approach. I said that I guessed we needed to discuss the matter with the principal and headed toward his office. To my surprise, he passed me in a fast walk, headed in the same direction. When we arrived, several other people joined us in conference with the principal and two assistant principals.

I began to say that I hoped this wasn't going on with other parents, but before I could get out any more words this coach began to blurt a string of inappropriate adjectives. Rather than reacting, I simply looked him in the face, instantly recognizing this as the work of the enemy. The principal finally spoke up, telling the coach that he was out of order and could lose his job for this type of behavior. His fury was diffused, the principal stated that the matter would be discussed later on, and everyone went back to work.

I was already scheduled to be out of town the next day—in Hickory, North Carolina, for some training with spiritual mentors Pastor Steve and Balinda Deitz. As it turned out, I had a wonderful time training the young leaders in Hickory concerning leadership. During my ninety-minute drive back to Greensboro, the Lord began to speak to me about apologizing for having offended this coach. Surprised that God was asking this of me, I objected, "Lord, he was the one who cussed me out, so why do I have to apologize?" Almost immediately the words of Isaiah 1:19–20, familiar to me since my college days, popped into my mind: "'If you are willing and obedient, You shall eat the good the land; But if you refuse and rebel, You shall be devoured by the sword.' For the mouth of the LORD has spoken." Balinda Deitz, whom I call "Mom Deitz," says, "Love is key in leadership; we must love regardless of the cost. We may not always understand, but we can stand firm in every trial. In order to love, we must at all times patiently forgive." She also goes on to say, "We cannot truly love a person until we experience their shortcomings, faults, and sins and be willing to forgive and love them to life."

I knew I would have to apologize, so when I arrived at school the next day I went to the coach duty station before school started, approached him, stated that I was sorry for having offended him, and asked whether he would forgive me. A look of amazement on his face, he responded in the affirmative. I shook his hand and went on to carry out my morning duties, assuming that this would be the end of my conversation with the Lord concerning this coach.

Very early the following morning, however, while I was walking back to the house after working out at the school track, the Lord began telling me to pray for the football team to have a successful season. My incredulous response: "Lord, I don't want to do that. Even though it's my alma mater, I don't want this coach to have a good season." The Lord repeated that I was to pray for him and the team, and I conceded. This is what I prayed: "Lord, let the Grimsley football team have the best year they ever had." Guess what happened? They experienced their best season since 1960, making it all the way to the state 4A championship. Wow! We as leaders must remember that God's ways are always higher than our own. In this instance, I'm convinced that God wanted to show this coach how much He loved him and needed a willing vessel. Leadership is all about being tenderhearted in responding to the Lord. As an unknown author has reflected, if we're unwilling to yield to the Lord we have no business leading.

My friend John Sheppard from my college days allowed his daughter Hannah to share her experience in servant leadership. She says,

> My passion for excellence guides my daily life and naturally leads to positions of leadership. I do everything to the absolute best of my ability and with integrity, from academics to athletics to art. My motto is to set goals high and strive for perfection, knowing that I will meet excellence as a result. I believe that true leadership is developed through serving others. I meet and overcome challenges, while encouraging others to do the same.
>
> My love for sports, such as soccer and basketball, has provided the perfect platform to do exactly that. As team captain for both sports, I have learned precisely what it means to give my best effort, despite difficulty while pushing teammates to be the best they can be. Basketball has taught me to appreciate both ends of the

playing spectrum, from sitting on the bench all season in 10th grade to never leaving the court as a senior. This experience has taught me how to relate to my teammates at all different levels of performance and experience. Basketball has also shown me what it means to be mentally tough. Not overly tall or strong, I have learned to meet physical challenges that have taught me to push through physical discomfort and have provided me with the knowledge that I can go beyond what my body feels capable of. This has also given me mental toughness.

My determination to try new things and not quit has taught me time management as well. I juggle many activities and responsibilities, including student government, honors and dual credit classes, and two varsity sports simultaneously for two seasons. I am also not afraid to enter new situations alone.

Halfway through middle school I transferred from homeschooling all my life to the largest private school in Virginia. The experience was scary, but it taught me how to accept change and be out of my comfort zone. Since then, new situations, such as summer camps in other states and tryouts for AAU teams where I know almost no one, have excited me. My determination has rewarded me with mental toughness, time management skills, and courage in new situations. My passion and determination in every situation have developed me to become the leader and servant I am today. I desire to contribute and be a part.

Hannah has learned at a young age some very important leadership attributes. In 1 Timothy 4:12 Paul counsels another younger leader, "Let no one despise your youth, but be an example to the believers in word, in conduct, in love, in spirit, in faith, in purity," Hannah is an elevating, effective leader because she is clearly knowledgeable about serving others.

Elevate Leadership Moment:

At JP Stevens I organized lines for lift trucks to make shift changes more efficient. I served as a distribution supervisor at JP Stevens, and at the time of its merger with Westpoint Pepperell we became the largest bedroom accessories textile manufacturing company in the world. This warehouse environment was very fast-paced; we were continually shipping out goods as fast as possible. The orders came from all of the major retail stores that sold comforters and bedroom accessories.

I was the second-shift supervisor and had twenty employees under my care and leadership. One regular complaint I would hear from employees at the change of shifts had to do with their difficulty locating their machines. Each picker or locator was assigned a picking machine. All pickers and locators were on a production schedule, with each picker having to pull at least 600–700 comforters and accessories each night and each locator expected to pick up a pallet of goods and store the inventory inside our large warehouses. I began to notice how much time was being lost because first-shift employees would leave the machines all over the huge warehouses, making it difficult for the second shift to get underway. I spoke regularly to first-shift supervisors, but to no avail.

Finally, I asked permission of my department manager, Reid Corrier, to come up with a system to make shift changes more efficient for all shifts. The department manager gave me the green light, asking the maintenance department to cooperate with me on this project. I discovered a huge open space next to the supervisory offices in one of the newly built warehouses. I arranged to have the lanes and machines numbered in numerical order, lined up the machines with heavy-duty tape, and had trucks lined up and parked in a single location so that when employees would arrive at work they would know exactly where to go to retrieve their assigned machines. Before this system was put in place, employees would regularly spend fifteen, twenty, or even thirty minutes looking for their machines; with the new system they were up and running within five. This system increased efficiency for all shifts, and my colleagues, managers, and other distribution employees were grateful for this simple but innovative idea. These are the kinds of innovations that help leaders excel and glorify God in their work.

Elevate Facts:

Friendliness is a key component of serving, and a smile communicates in every language and culture.

Accommodating others will help facilitate smooth interaction.

Creativity paves the way to serve and help people with excellence and skill.

Tune—staying tuned for creative ways to serve.

Seven S's of Servanthood:

1. Stop to listen for others' concerns and needs.
2. Sincere—be genuinely concerned and listen without interrupting.
3. Strengths—know your own strengths so you can serve most effectively.
4. Stand on the solid rock of the truth that serving is the way to greatness.
5. Staying strong in the Lord is the key to longevity and vitality.
6. Sensitivity is vital for awareness of unique ways in which to serve particular people.
7. Standard of service must be elevated to help people realize how much we value them and how much God loves them.

In Paul's words in 2 Timothy 2:24–26, "A servant of the Lord must not quarrel but be gentle to all, able to teach, patient, in humility correcting those who are in opposition, if God perhaps will grant them repentance, so that they may know the truth, and that they may come to their senses and escape the snare of the devil, having been taken captive by him to do his will." People are easily entrapped by lies, and Satan is the father of lies.

Elevate Questions:

1. Are you serving your family through acts of kindness?
2. How can you become a more effective leader?
3. According to 1 Corinthians 4:1–2, what does God require of stewards?
4. According to Deuteronomy 30:19, in what area does God give us a choice?
5. What did Coach Rex have to do that was humbling with regard to the other coach?
6. How did Coach Rex's innovation improve workflow for the entire company?
7. What is the key ingredient in being a great leader?

Leaders' Prayer:

Father help us maintain a servant heart in our leadership, recognizing this is a major kingdom principle that you desire in all of us. Help us serve to honor and please you more than anyone or anything in Jesus's name, Amen.

I'm glad you've decided to join me on this journey of reading, learning, and growing in your leadership. We have a duty and responsibility to warn and help people come to know the Way, the Truth, and the Life in Christ. In Romans 16:17–18 Paul gives us a clear directive: "Now I urge you, brethren, note those who cause divisions and offenses, contrary to the doctrine which you learned, and avoid them. For those who are such do not serve our Lord Jesus Christ, but their own belly, and by smooth words and flattering speech deceive the hearts of the simple." Unfortunately, some have an agenda that is based on deception, twisting the truth, and all-out lawlessness. Leaders have a responsibility to do what is right, to be merciful, and to walk in humility, avoiding the toxic spirit of pride, hatred, and bitterness that is a killer of effective leadership. We who follow Christ must not fall for the lies of the enemy or be swayed by the opinion of a few who insist that Christians shouldn't be involved in governing our country.

Politics may be defined as "the activities associated with the governance of a country or other area, especially the debate or conflict among individuals or parties having or hoping to achieve power." The first and second amendments to the United States Constitution are statements of rights crafted by the forefathers of the United States of America, who leaned heavily on the Bible for insight and direction in forging this country. We must stay with our biblical foundation and pass along our freedoms, including those of speech and religion, to our children's children. We must be involved in every sphere that influences our nation. When we allow ourselves to become complacent and sit back, we allow lawlessness to prevail—and then we wonder why America has been on this course of destruction. We must turn America back to God and let our voice be heard all across our land.

Now that you've read this book it's time to elevate. In Paul's words in Philippians 3:14, "I press toward the goal for the prize of the upward call of God in Christ Jesus." The Hebrew word *aliyah* means to go on an upward journey. As Billy Graham challenges us, "Who will rise to the pressing need in today's world for inspired leadership? Who will rise to its high calling and are willing to carry its weight?

Who will determine to deepen and expand their capacities and effectiveness?"

Leadership is no cakewalk, but in 2 Timothy 2:3 Paul calls upon each of us as a leader to "endure hardship as a good soldier of Jesus Christ." As Scripture makes clear in Job 5:7, "man is born to trouble, As the sparks fly upward." Everyone experiences personal tragedies and inevitable grief, but leaders bear all of these on behalf of others, along with the sometimes agonizing weight of knowing the degree to which their decisions, attitudes, and actions may affect others.

We as leaders must stop isolating ourselves and must instead insulate ourselves with accountability partners who also serve as our prayer partners. I personally appreciate two couples, Gary and Jill Gramlich and Peter and Debbie Udall, for their support during that rough period in my life after I had experienced a concussion and when I was enduring setbacks having to do with anger, memory deficits, and family challenges. Their support and prayers have helped in more ways than I could ever have imagined. Having friends to hold one accountable is priceless, and leaders who want to elevate their leadership must submit themselves to constructive criticism.

In my journey to accountability I was asked the question "Why are you so defensive?"—to which I quickly replied, "I am not defensive!" This was my moment of truth realization. I had my guard up and was ready to defend myself and refute virtually anything the accountability team had to say. It was indeed a rude awakening for me to realize that if I wanted help I would need to let down my guard and be vulnerable and open to adjusting my attitude concerning key issues.

The next session dealt with the situation in my home of origin; I had been unaware growing up that my father's heavy expectations were unrealistic. This accountability team helped me see that I can't expect of my family today what my father expected of me and my siblings. We as leaders must allow the Lord to change unhealthy thought patterns that might otherwise be perpetuated from generation to generation. This session resulted in a major breakthrough as well.

In the next session, which I'll call "Sparks Flying," the three of us husbands were at a local restaurant discussing politics in general, along with the possibility of my wife's becoming involved. I wasn't at this point thrilled about the suggestion and became quite angry when the subject was mentioned. I didn't realize how selfish I was being in wanting everything to be centered around myself—a major blind spot. I became overly vocal in this public place, inciting Gary to follow suit, even though all the while I could see the holy fear of

God moving through these two men of God.

During that session God warned me about my willful attitude, and I realized at that moment that the Lord was serious about Vickie and me stepping up to His call; I needed to give Vickie my full support in the areas toward which the Lord was leading our family. Weeks later I was invited to work on my writing in Dubois, Wyoming, with friends Dave and Liz Furman, who own a motel right next to the Wind- River. While praying and writing next to this inspiring and beautiful river, I began to sense a holy call to give my full support to my wife's involvement in government. Vickie and I had been united in terms of what God was calling us to do, but the enemy had launched several attacks in an attempt to prevent us from moving forward into this divine destiny during this season of our lives. With the help of the accountability team I have come to see how blessed I am to have such an amazing woman of God as my wife. We as husbands and fathers must endeavor to empower those we love and lead by our actions, to serve with excellence, doing all we can to help our families succeed.

I believe that God is warning leaders that business is not "as usual" when it comes to our dealings with the Lord; He is calling us to a higher level of character and engagement. Let us learn the lesson that pride can disqualify us from leadership eligibility. Eli allowed sin to go unchecked; his failure to correct and remove his sons from priestly leadership precipitated divine judgment upon Israel. Nebuchadnezzar of Babylon had to be removed from his throne and spend time with animals. He lived in the fields, ate grass like a cow, and had feathers like a bird. The Persian Belshazzar didn't learn from his predecessor and lost his life for his willful rebellion against God. God desires that we excel in our leadership, and we do this by daily seeking Him, humbling ourselves, loving mercy, and doing what is right in His sight.

CONCLUSION

Reflecting back on each of the seven steps for elevating effective leadership, it is imperative for us first to acknowledge that people in leadership positions often think they can lead effectively and have a lasting positive impact without love. God, on the other hand, clearly tells us that if we lack love we are *nothing*. Love brings an element of God's nature into our leadership, and whatever God says is the final word because He is God; as such, He sees all that we do and knows the motives underlying our attitudes, intentions, speech, behaviors, and actions. If we hurt people for personal gain, we will give an account to God.

With regard to encouragement, while we do need the help and support of family and friends, if we rely solely on them we'll find that they'll eventually let us down; that's a given of human nature. Going to God for encouragement, on the other hand, will infuse us with a continuous and consistent source of strength. Being in God's presence and interacting with the Lord with provide the ability to advance forward into our divine destiny.

I have learned from experience, from reading, and from observing leaders that attitude is a seemingly minor component that makes an incomparable difference. Our attitude determines where we will go in life and what doors God will open for us. If we allow environment, media, and other secular influences to dictate our attitude, our chances of soaring to make a lasting kingdom impact will be minimized. We are called to cultivate an attitude of gratitude, to be thankful for each new day God gives us. My challenge to you is to make some attitude adjustments.

Be warned: this is going to require that you change some patterns of thinking that are contrary to God's. His ways are infinitely higher than our own, and when we begin to align ourselves with Him we will with the Spirit's help elevate our attitudes. This will result in being an elevating effective leader for God's glory.

Step four, that of delegating, necessitates slowing down to explain in detail what we expect from those we're leading, as well as inspecting what it is we expect and leading our team by example through modeling and demonstration. My friend Kevin Hunt, who is originally from North Carolina and now lives and works in Augusta, Georgia, learned the art of delegation. Kevin was the head football coach and he recognized that the players on his school's team wanted the current assistant coach to become the head coach. Being secure in his leadership, Kevin empowered the assistant coach, allowing him to influence the team from a position of authority. Kevin also mentored this coach to be a better leader and appointed him to the defensive coordinator that season. The coach later became the head football coach at the school. Kevin made a tough situation a win-win for the entire program. This is a prime example of delegating and empowering leaders.

The endurance principle is about refusing to quit, even and especially when things heat up and moving forward becomes a tough slog. During my tenure within a school district I had a tough time with the leader who oversaw our department. This person was clearly incompetent in terms of understanding safety procedures and in the basics of handling people. I cannot tell you the countless times I wanted to quit. His ineptitude resulted in my being injured on the job, and he often targeted me for unnecessary confrontational conversations in his office. Through prayer I was able to endure all of the challenges he put before me.

At the end of the school year my co-workers asked how I had managed to keep going, despite having had to take so much from this administrator. How had I kept myself composed? My unequivocal answer: God! I had developed a daily discipline of praying over the situation for *at least* seven minutes or more, and this helped sustain me during one of the hardest times in my life. Spending consistent time with God will infuse you with strength, hope, purpose, vision, understanding, wisdom, and self-control.

I have learned from many years of *not* being ready the vital importance of preparedness. This life skill has enhanced my leadership, and I believe in this principle so much that I have written about readiness in two of the three books I have written; in each of them I have dedicated a chapter to the topic. I challenge you to spiritually prepare yourself in every way by becoming a student of God's Word, to physically get and stay in good condition to equip you to handle any situation that may warrant physical strength and stamina, and to mentally stay abreast of written material that aligns with your calling. Emotional preparation equips you to negotiate those inevitable triggers based on past experiences that can derail and disqualify your leadership. In other words, be ready for anything at any time. God's Word enjoins us to watch and pray; this means being ever vigilant to the guidance of the Holy Spirit, being dressed in our battle gear and in the mode of praying in the Spirit.

The last step of leadership is servanthood. Our Lord Jesus made it clear that greatness in His kingdom is built upon a servant foundation. Too many well-intentioned leaders have gotten the priorities backward. True leadership consists of doing all we can to help those under our influence to have better lives. Servanthood entails giving up what is convenient for ourselves in favor of convenience for those *we serve in our leadership capacity*.

Servanthood for you might look like knowing that it will be a challenge for your neighbor to shovel snow in bitter temperatures, while you could make short work of the task with your snow blower. Or like assisting a single parent in figuring out how to arrange for the care of her children when you have the means and ability to help. Servanthood for you might entail prioritizing your wife's preferences over your own. I challenge you to think ahead and to show consideration for your loved ones and for those others you serve, to do all you can to make every day a masterpiece *for them*.

It is my prayer that you may capture the essence of the leadership principles I have gleaned from my experiences, observations, and research in order to become a person who leads others effectively, and that you will pass along what you have learned to the younger generation, doing your part to elevate and perpetuate effective leadership into the future in Jesus's name.

My challenge to you is to be a leader who breathes life and confidence into those you are called to serve. Genuine concern about each individual's well-being and a demonstrated enthusiasm for their unique giftedness will go a long way toward enhancing your effectiveness.

I remember that as a child my friends and I would ride our bicycles everywhere—often at breakneck speed. We would take turns playing Follow the Leader, a game that often entailed crazy antics and unexpected twists and turns as we zigzagged our way through the maze that was our inner city neighborhood. I found this fun and exciting because we never knew whether the leader would go straight, shoot to the right, or veer left. Wisely or unwisely, we implicitly trusted one another to lead us through safe passages. We as leaders function best when we follow the Holy Spirit, in turn guiding those who follow us in the ways of truth and righteousness. When we hit a dead end we back up and correct the course for all involved. We are ambassadors representing our King.

I challenge you to be a passionate leader, loving God first and foremost and, secondarily loving your family with passionate affection. I challenge you not to take yourself too seriously and to be willing from time to time, alone or in the presence of your followers, to laugh at yourself. I challenge you to lead with integrity in every facet of your life. Integrity (*tom* in the Hebrew) is about completeness; it is the quality of being honest, of having and following strong moral principles, and of being morally upright, sincere, truthful, and trustworthy. I challenge you to promote and stand up for biblical values, thereby influencing the culture in which you find yourself to reach new heights in Christ as you and those you influence learn to speak the truth in love. Don't allow personal ambition, convenience, greed, or prejudice to steer you away from doing what is pleasing in God's sight.

I challenge you to love more passionately, encourage more regularly, align your attitude to the principles of Scripture engrained in your heart, delegate deliberately to faithful and capable people, endure hardships like a soldier, and be ready at a moment's notice for anything, willing to serve God in any way you can to advance His kingdom and doing your best to make your family a priority. I challenge you to do all of this with an eye laser focused on the glory of God.

Allow me to remind you that we are engaged in a very real war between good and evil; in our great country there is a hidden agenda to thwart anyone who dares to represent and proclaim the name of Jesus. The freedom to practice our religion unimpeded is a gift from God to all Americans. Far from taking that gift for granted, we need to be faithful and vigilant, doing all we can to ensure that it remains intact and flourishes; we must be intentional in praying for guidance to bring the message of hope and love to all people, and we need to be good stewards, ensuring through our generosity that the Church and its ministries are equipped to advance the gospel throughout the earth and into every sphere that influences the hearts and minds of people. We must remember to lead in humility, bearing ever in mind that pride and anger slam shut the door of love and unity. Finally, we are called to redeem the time; none of us is promised a tomorrow, and while we have today we are to let people know that God loves them and has an amazing purpose and plan for their lives.

In the words of 2 Chronicles 29:11, "My sons, do not be negligent now, for the LORD has chosen you to stand before Him, to serve Him, and that you should minister to Him and burn incense." The Lord has chosen *you* to stand in His presence to minister to Him through your ministrations to others, to lead people in worship, and to present offerings to Him.

Let's rise up, then, and be all that God has called and destined us to be. Don't succumb to fear or intimidation, since God—who has promised to be with you wherever you go—has *commanded* you, as He did Joshua, to be strong and courageous. God is more than capable of producing in your life a harvest of fruit beyond your wildest dreams or comprehension, to astound you and those around you by what He chooses to do with your gifts, to use you as a conduit for disseminating to others the bounties of His unmerited grace and favor. Give your time, talent, and treasure to help deliver those who are headed toward destruction. In the words of Proverbs 24:11, "Deliver those who are drawn toward death, And hold back those stumbling to the slaughter."

Keep your leadership on the cutting edge by continuing to learn and grow in Christ. We're reminded in Ecclesiastes 10:10 that "if the ax is dull, And one does not sharpen the edge, Then he must use more strength; But wisdom brings success." Leadership is a continuous process of sharpening our lives, of honing our "edge" for maximum effectiveness. If you aren't learning you aren't growing, and if you aren't growing you are failing to access and appropriate all of the ability God has placed within you.

As God reminded His prophet in Jeremiah 1:5, "Before I formed you in the womb I knew you; Before you were born I sanctified you; I ordained you a prophet to the nations." Our callings and leadership spheres differ, yes, but God knew each one of us before we were born and has implanted within us unique abilities that enable us to accomplish precisely what He has in mind for us.

The legendary coach Bear Bryant once commented that "a great leader must have an intense work ethic. There's just no other way around it. If a leader is lazy, then he is not a leader." Coach Bryant delineates five key leadership principles each of us does well to keep in mind: (1) expect the unexpected, (2) be prepared every day, (3) keep your poise, (4) play with confidence and class, and (5) remember that it takes personal sacrifice to be successful.

In closing, let's take a look at the apostle Paul's assessment in 1 Timothy 3:1–7 for his younger protégé Timothy of the qualities that enable successful leadership within the Church:

> This is a faithful saying: If a man desires the position of a bishop, he desires a good work. A bishop then must be blameless, the husband of one wife, temperate, sober-minded, of good behavior, hospitable, able to teach; not given to wine, not violent, not greedy for money, but gentle, not quarrelsome, not covetous; one who rules his own house well, having his children in submission with all reverence (for if a man does not know how to rule his own house, how will he take care of the church of God?); not a novice, lest being puffed up with pride he fall into the same condemnation as the devil. Moreover he must have a good testimony among those who are outside, lest he fall into reproach and the snare of the devil.

We as leaders must recognize that we need God's help to lead effectively just as Solomon recognized in 1 Kings 3:9, "Give to Your servant an understanding heart to judge Your people, that I may discern between good and evil. For who is able to judge this great people of Yours?"

Leaders' Prayer:

Father, I come humbly to the throne of grace yearning for Spirit enablement to align my life more and more closely with your agenda. Lord, please look down from heaven and bring me into unity with your heart. Elevate my thinking so that I may behold more of your nature; reveal to my heart more and more of who you are. Hear my cries on behalf of those brokenhearted individuals, known or unknown to me, within my sphere of influence. I repent of sinful ways; help me to wake up from my stupor so I can hear what you are speaking in this hour. Help me to understand and resonate with what it is that breaks your heart. Lord, please bring times of refreshing, renewal, and revival to us, your people. We are in desperate need of your powerful presence. Jesus, help us to glorify the Father and make His name known wherever you send us. Help me to love and reflect your nature to every person I meet.

Father, I pray the words of Daniel 1:17 over my own and others' leadership. May the qualities of these exemplary young men be exemplified in our own time in myself and in us: "As for these four young men, God gave them knowledge and skill in all literature and wisdom; And Daniel had understanding in all visions and dreams."

Lord, we ask for unusual aptitude for understanding every aspect of literature and wisdom. Father, we ask for special ability to interpret the meanings of visions, dreams, and the times in which we are living. Lord, gift us with knowledge and sound judgment so that we may know how to serve effectively in the places to which you lead us. Help us to learn the languages of other cultures so that we can communicate your truth effectively in whatever setting we find ourselves. And Lord, because we live for you, help us to be many times more capable in our leadership. Father, give us favor with those we serve and with whom we work. We are confident that you, who began a good work in us, will carry it on to completion until the day of Christ Jesus. In Jesus's name, Amen.